INTERNET THEORY, TECHNOLOGY AND APPLICATIONS

CYBERSECURITY AND INFORMATION SECURITY AT DEPOSITORY INSTITUTIONS

SELECTED ASSESSMENTS

INTERNET THEORY, TECHNOLOGY AND APPLICATIONS

Additional books in this series can be found on Nova's website under the Series tab.

Additional e-books in this series can be found on Nova's website under the e-book tab.

INTERNET THEORY, TECHNOLOGY AND APPLICATIONS

CYBERSECURITY AND INFORMATION SECURITY AT DEPOSITORY INSTITUTIONS

SELECTED ASSESSMENTS

LAUREN HUBBARD
EDITOR

nova publishers
New York

Library of Congress Cataloging-in-Publication Data

ISBN: 978-1-63484-285-3

Published by Nova Science Publishers, Inc. † New York

CONTENTS

PREFACE

Depository institutions experienced cyber attacks in recent years that are estimated to have resulted in hundreds of millions of dollars in losses. Depository institution regulators (the Office of the Comptroller of the Currency, the Board of Governors of the Federal Reserve, the Federal Deposit Insurance Corporation, and NCUA) oversee information security at these institutions and Treasury coordinates protection of the financial sector. The objectives of this book include examining how regulators oversee institutions' efforts to mitigate cyber threats; and sources of and efforts by agencies to share cyber threat information. This book also assesses the effectiveness of the corporation's controls in protecting the confidentiality, integrity, and availability of its financial systems and information.

In: Cybersecurity and Information Security … ISBN: 978-1-63484-285-3
Editor: Lauren Hubbard

Chapter 1

Cybersecurity: Bank and Other Depository Regulators Need Better Data Analytics and Depository Institutions Want More Usable Threat Information*

United States Government Accountability Office

Why GAO Did This Study

Depository institutions experienced cyber attacks in recent years that are estimated to have resulted in hundreds of millions of dollars in losses. Depository institution regulators (the Office of the Comptroller of the Currency, the Board of Governors of the Federal Reserve, the Federal Deposit Insurance Corporation, and NCUA) oversee information security at these institutions and Treasury coordinates protection of the financial sector.

The objectives of this report include examining (1) how regulators oversee institutions' efforts to mitigate cyber threats, and (2) sources of and efforts by agencies to share cyber threat information. GAO collected and analyzed cyber security studies from private-sector sources. GAO reviewed materials from selected IT examinations (based on regulator, institution size, and risk level).

* This is an edited, reformatted and augmented version of a United States Government Accountability Office publication, No. GAO-15-509, dated July 2015

GAO also held three forums with more than 50 members of financial institution industry associations who provided opinions on cyber threat information sharing.

What GAO Recommends

Congress should consider granting NCUA authority to examine third-party technology service providers for credit unions. In addition, regulators should explore ways to better collect and analyze data on trends in IT examination findings across institutions. In written comments on a draft of this report, the four regulators stated that they would take steps responsive to this recommendation.

What GAO Found

Regulators use a risk-based examination approach to oversee the adequacy of information security at depository institutions—banks, thrifts, and credit unions— but could better target future examinations by analyzing deficiencies across institutions. For information technology (IT) examinations, regulators adjust the level of scrutiny at each institution depending on the information they review, past examination results, and any IT changes. GAO reviewed 15 IT examinations and found that regulators generally reviewed institutions' policies, interviewed staff, and examined audits of information security practices. While the largest institutions were generally examined by IT experts, medium and smaller institutions were sometimes reviewed by examiners with little or no IT training. The regulators recognized that some IT training is necessary for all examiners, so each regulator had efforts under way to increase the number of their staff with IT expertise and conduct more training. GAO identified two areas for improvement:

- **Data analytics**. Regulators generally focused on IT systems at individual institutions but most lacked readily available information on deficiencies across the banking system. Although federal internal control standards call for organizations to have relevant, reliable, and timely information on activities, regulators were not routinely collecting IT security incident reports and examination deficiencies and classifying them by category of deficiency. Having such data would better enable regulators to identify and analyze trends across institutions and use that analysis to better target areas for review at institutions.

- **Oversight authority**. Bank regulators directly address the risks posed to their regulated institutions from third-party technology service providers, but the National Credit Union Administration (NCUA) lacks this authority. Cyber risks affecting a depository institution can arise from weaknesses in the security practices of third parties that process information or provide other IT services to the institution. Bank regulators routinely conduct examinations of service providers' information security. Authorizing NCUA to routinely conduct such examinations could help it better ensure that the service providers for credit unions also follow sound information security practices.

Depository institutions obtain cyber threat information from multiple sources, including federal entities such as the Department of the Treasury (Treasury). Representatives from more than 50 financial institutions told GAO that obtaining adequate information on cyber threats from federal sources was challenging. Information viewed as most helpful for assessing threats and protecting systems included details on attacks other institutions experienced. To help address these needs, Treasury has various efforts under way to obtain such information and confidentially share it with other institutions. The department formed a special group that works with other law enforcement and intelligence agencies to obtain declassified information and share it with financial institutions in a series of circulars. Treasury staff also participate in Department of Homeland Security groups that monitor cyber incidents and work with a center that provides cyber threat information to thousands of financial institutions.

ABBREVIATIONS

ATM	automated teller machine
DDOS	distributed denial of service
DHS	Department of Homeland Security
DOJ	Department of Justice
FBI	Federal Bureau of Investigation
FBIIC	Financial and Banking Information Infrastructure Committee

FDIC	Federal Deposit Insurance Corporation
FFIEC	Federal Financial Institutions Examination Council
FinCEN	Financial Crimes Enforcement Network
FS-ISAC	Financial Services Information Sharing and Analysis Center
FSOC	Financial Stability Oversight Council
FSSCC	Financial Services Sector Coordinating Council for Critical Infrastructure
IT	information technology
NCCIC	National Cybersecurity and Communications Information Center
NCUA	National Credit Union Administration
OCC	Office of the Comptroller of the Currency
OCIP	Office of Critical Infrastructure Protection and Compliance Policy

* * *

July 2, 2015

Congressional Requesters

Threats to the security of depository institutions' information have grown in frequency and sophistication. For instance, in 2012 and 2013, more than a dozen depository institutions sustained cyber attacks that prevented access to their public websites. In late 2014 a major U.S. depository institution experienced an intrusion that compromised personal information of tens of millions of customers. Depository institutions are estimated to have incurred hundreds of millions of dollars in losses from breaches in the systems of their corporate customers that allowed criminals to illegally transfer funds from the customer's bank accounts, and from frauds perpetrated against their automated teller machines (ATM), according to federal law enforcement sources.[1] Pervasive Internet use has revolutionized the way that nations, businesses, and individuals communicate and conduct many activities. While the benefits have been substantial, widespread connectivity also poses significant risks to computer systems, networks, and associated critical operations and key infrastructure. Depository institutions—including banks, thrifts, and credit unions—provide an array of products for their customers, all of which may be accessed or delivered through information technology (IT) platforms and channels that unauthorized individuals and organizations can access or use to interfere with an institution's operations. To combat these threats, depository institutions implemented information security to protect and secure systems and facilities that process and maintain information vital to their operations.

Such threats recently prompted the Financial Stability Oversight Council (FSOC) to highlight operational risk, and information security in particular, as worthy of heightened risk management and supervisory attention.[2] In its 2014 annual report, the council stated that mitigating evolving information security threats, effectively managing incidents, and promoting recovery efforts from such events were critical to maintaining public confidence and reducing financial risk. Since 1997, we have included federal information security on our list of high-risk issues facing the federal government, and in 2015 we included efforts to protect the privacy of personally identifiable information.[3]

In response to high-profile cyber attacks on U.S. institutions, you requested that we study the risks depository institutions face due to cyber attacks from criminal organizations and other illicit actors. This report examines (1) cyber attacks on U.S. depository institutions, including the types of threats, impacts, and protective measures taken; (2) the extent to which regulators oversee depository institutions' efforts to mitigate cyber threats; and (3) sources of cyber threat information and efforts by relevant federal agencies to share threat information with depository institutions.[4]

To obtain information on cyber threats, we reviewed studies by banking associations, consulting firms, and researchers about information security threats to depository institutions and how they defend themselves from attacks. We summarized studies by banking associations and consulting firms on the costs and effects of cyber attacks. We selected these studies based on a literature search. We reviewed the methodologies employed in the studies, and determined that the studies were sufficiently reliable for our purposes. We reviewed the websites of selected institutions to determine the extent to which they provide information to customers on protecting themselves from threats. We selected these institutions based on their asset size and likely large customer base. Finally, we interviewed information security vendors, bank regulators, federal law enforcement agencies, and industry groups.[5] The information security vendors we interviewed included Battelle, Early Warning Services, the National Cyber-Forensics and Training Alliance, Plante Moran, Prolexic, Trustwave, and Verafin.

To obtain information on the extent to which regulators have overseen actions to mitigate cyber threats, we analyzed examination data from 2013 for 15 banks and credit unions that included a sample of 12 institutions (1 large institution and 11 medium and small institutions) and an additional 3 medium and small institutions that a regulator selected for our review because their examinations covered IT activities. 6 We also reviewed examinations conducted in 2013 of seven selected IT service providers to determine the extent to which these companies were supervised for information security risks. As criteria for these reviews, we reviewed the mandate of the bank regulators to supervise their member institutions, under which they conduct examinations to ensure that these institutions are conducting their operations in ways to ensure their safety and soundness. We reviewed guidance issued by bank regulators since June 2011 to examine the extent to which the guidance addresses recent prominent threats. We reviewed aggregated data provided by the bank regulators on the number of bank IT examinations and the number of deficiencies regulators identified in the examinations, among other data elements. We also assessed the regulators' efforts to collect and analyze examination data against relevant federal internal control standards.[7] To determine the reliability of these data, we reviewed information about the systems used to collect the data and agency statements on how the data were prepared. We determined that data were sufficiently reliable for our purposes.

To examine how depository institutions receive and share information about information security threats, and the type of information they need to adequately prepare for these threats, we interviewed officials from 2 smaller institutions, one of which was selected from our sample of 12 institutions whose examination materials we reviewed, and also obtained views from more than 50 large, medium, and small depository and other financial-sector institutions that participated in forums organized for us by financial trade associations. We reviewed the information security websites and notices of federal agencies to determine the extent to which they provide information to depository institutions or the public about information security threats or protection steps. We also reviewed the Suspicious Activity Report—the form that financial sector institutions use to report suspicious activity to the Department of the Treasury (Treasury)—to determine the extent to which it captures cyber-related information. Lastly, we reviewed and summarized information in prior GAO reports about challenges and recommendations for improved information sharing for information security. See appendix I for a full description of our scope and methodology.

We conducted this performance audit from February 2014 to July 2015 in accordance with generally accepted government auditing standards. Those standards require that we plan and perform the audit to obtain sufficient, appropriate evidence to provide a reasonable basis for our findings and conclusions based on our audit objectives. We believe that the evidence obtained provides a reasonable basis for our findings and conclusions based on our audit objectives.

BACKGROUND

Depository institutions increasingly rely on IT systems to maintain records of their assets and liabilities and conduct many other activities, such as maintaining information on customer deposits, investments, and loans. In addition, depository institutions have electronic connections to various payment systems that link institutions to one another and to customers. Examples of these systems and networks are major credit card networks, the automated clearing-house operators, and ATM networks that permit consumers to access their funds worldwide. Several other payment systems, such as the Clearing House Interbank Payments System and Fedwire, support larger-value payments.

Certain electronic banking services that depository institutions offer to business customers can expose both parties to risks because the transactions typically enable the exchange of confidential customer information and the transfer of funds. These services include loan application and approval and payments between corporate customers. Depository institutions also provide services to retail customers that can expose them to cyber threats. For example, many institutions allow customers to conduct transactions on websites, including transferring funds and making payments to third parties. A growing number of institutions allow such transactions to originate on mobile devices.

Depository institutions make extensive use of technology service providers that supply them with IT processing, management, and security. Institutions can outsource many areas of operations, including the origination, processing, and settlement of payments and financial transactions; information processing related to customer accounts; fiduciary and trading activities; security monitoring and testing; system development and maintenance, network operations; and call centers. The ability to contract for IT services typically enables an institution to offer customers enhanced services and use infrastructure comparable to that of larger institutions without the expenses involved in owning the technology or maintaining staff to deploy and operate it.

Overview of Responsibilities and Oversight Functions of Bank Regulators

Federal bank regulators have responsibility for ensuring the safety and soundness of the institutions they oversee, protecting federal deposit insurance funds, promoting stability in financial markets, and enforcing compliance with applicable consumer protection laws (see table 1).

Table 1. Federal Bank Regulators and Their Functions

Agency	Basic function
Office of the Comptroller of the Currency (OCC)	Charters and supervises national banks and federal savings associations and federally chartered branches and agencies of foreign banks
Board of Governors of the Federal Reserve System (Federal Reserve)	Supervises state-chartered banks that opt to be members of the Federal Reserve System,bank holding companies, savings and loan holding companies and the nondepository institution subsidiaries of those organizations, and nonbank financial companies designated for Federal Reserve supervision by the Financial Stability Oversight Council
Federal Deposit Insurance Corporation (FDIC)	Supervises FDIC-insured, state-chartered banks that are not members of the Federal Reserve System, as well as federally insured state savings banks and savings associations; insures the deposits of all banks and savings associations that are approvedfor federal deposit insurance; and resolves all failed insured banks and savings associations and certain nonbank financial companies
National Credit Union Administration (NCUA)	Charters and supervises federally chartered credit unions and insures deposits in federally chartered and the majority of state-chartered credit unions

Source: GAO. | GAO-15-509.

To achieve these goals, the regulators assess the financial condition of the institutions and monitor compliance with applicable banking laws and regulations. The regulators also develop and publish guidance to assist (1) regulated entities in fulfilling requirements, addressing specific threats, or mitigating identified risks; and (2) their examiners in carrying out their reviews of the adequacy of the protections implemented by the entities they regulate. (We discuss guidance for information security activities in greater detail later in this report.)

Federal Efforts to Address Critical Infrastructure

Various laws and policies established roles and responsibilities for federal agencies to enhance the cyber and physical security of critical public and private infrastructures, including the financial services sector.[8] These include the Homeland Security Act of 2002, Presidential Policy Directive 21, and the National Infrastructure Protection Plan.[9]

The Homeland Security Act of 2002 created the Department of Homeland Security (DHS). The act assigned the department the following critical infrastructure protection responsibilities: (1) developing a comprehensive national plan for securing the key resources and critical infrastructures of the United States; (2) assisting the development and promotion of private-sector best practices to secure critical infrastructure; and (3) disseminating, as appropriate, information to assist deterrence, prevention, and preemption of, or response to, terrorist attacks.[10]

DHS has been designated as the principal federal agency to lead, integrate and coordinate the implementation of efforts to protect cybercritical infrastructures and key resources. In carrying out its responsibilities, DHS established the United States Computer Emergency Readiness Team in 2003 to defend against and help to respond to cyber attacks on executive branch agencies and share information and collaborate with state and local governments, industry, and international partners. DHS also established the National Cybersecurity and Communications Integration Center (NCCIC) in 2010 to share information from federal agencies; state, local, tribal, and territorial governments; and the private sector, including international stakeholders.[11] In addition, the presidential policy directive identifies lead federal agencies, referred to as sector-specific agencies, which are responsible for coordinating critical infrastructure protection efforts with the public and private stakeholders in their sectors. For the financial sector, Treasury is tasked with prioritizing and coordinating the protection of the critical infrastructure in the sector (including depository institutions) and providing, supporting, or facilitating technical assistance to identify vulnerabilities and help mitigate incidents.

Federal activities to protect the nation's critical infrastructure often are conducted in conjunction with private-sector owners and operators of this infrastructure, as described in the National Infrastructure Protection Plan.

For each infrastructure sector, government coordinating councils—composed of federal, state, local, or tribal agencies—develop plans and oversee protection activities. For banking and other financial services, the

Financial and Banking Information Infrastructure Committee (FBIIC) is charged with improving coordination and communication among financial regulators, enhancing the resiliency of the financial sector, and promoting public-private partnerships. It is chaired by Treasury's Assistant Secretary for Financial Institutions and its 18 members represent federal regulators and associations of state regulators. Similarly, the Financial Services Sector Coordinating Council for Critical Infrastructure Protection and Homeland Security (FSSCC)—a group of private-sector institutions that includes more than 40 banks (investment, commercial, and retail) and credit unions—assists DHS in infrastructure protection activities for the financial sector. This council represents a primary point of contact for federal agencies to plan the entire range of infrastructure protection activities, including those associated with mitigating cyber threats.

The Financial Crimes Enforcement Network (FinCEN), a bureau within Treasury, is tasked with safeguarding the U.S. financial system from money laundering, terrorist financing, and other abuses. Depository institutions must file Suspicious Activity Reports with FinCEN when a transaction involving or aggregating at least $5,000 relates to a known or suspected violation of any law or regulation, including cyber attacks.[12] Suspicious activity reporting is one component of broader anti-moneylaundering programs that depository institutions implement. Bank regulators examine institutions for compliance with Suspicious Activity Report requirements as part of their regularly scheduled on-site examinations.

Finally, the Department of Justice (DOJ) and the Secret Service play an important role in addressing cyber crime (criminal activities that specifically target a computer or network for damage or infiltration). For example, it can be a crime to access ("hack") a computer without authorization to obtain information, to employ viruses or other malicious code to damage computers, or to use computers to conduct criminal activity such as fraud, identity theft, and copyright infringement, if those acts are committed with the necessary intent. Agencies in DOJ that focus on enforcing cyber crime violations include the Criminal Division, National Security Division, the U.S. Attorneys' Offices, and the Federal Bureau of Investigation (FBI). The Secret Service (a DHS agency) investigates crimes against the national financial system committed by criminals around the world and in cyberspace. State and local law enforcement organizations also have key responsibilities in addressing cyber crime.

Common Types of Cyber Threats and Sources of Attacks

Cyber threats can include targeted and untargeted attacks that may adversely affect computers, software, a network, an industry, or the Internet itself. The potential impact of these threats is amplified by the connectivity among information systems, the Internet, and other infrastructures. Table 2 provides descriptions of selected common types of cyber attacks. Information security vendors and technology service providers we interviewed stated that attack types were more frequently being combined. For instance, a denial-of-service attack could overwhelm an institution's IT system and wire fraud would not be detected while the system was unavailable. Additionally, very sophisticated threats—called advanced persistent threats—increasingly have been used to breach the information systems of government and commercial entities to obtain unauthorized access to data. Such intrusions can go undetected for long periods.

Table 2. Selected Common Types of Cyber Attacks

Type of exploit	Description
Denial-of-service	An attack that prevents or impairs the authorized use of networks, systems, or applications by exhausting resources.
Distributed denial-of-service	A variant of the denial-of-service attack that uses numerous hosts to perform the attack.
Advanced persistent threats	An attack, frequently associated with national actors, in which adversaries who possess sophisticated levels of expertise and significant resources pursue their objectives repeatedly over an extended period oftime and pose increasing risks.
Phishing	A digital form of social engineering that uses authentic-looking, but fake, e-mails to request information from users or direct them to a fake website that requests information. Spear phishing attacks are often used by individuals conducting targeted, rather than opportunistic, attacks.
Malware	Malicious software designed to carry out annoying or harmful actions. Once installed, malware often can masquerade as useful programs or be embedded into useful programs so that users are induced into activating the program and thus spreading the malware to other devices.
Botnet	A network of remotely controlled systems used to coordinate attacks and distribute malware, spam, and phishing scams.

Table 2. (Continued)

Type of exploit	Description
	Bots (short for robots) are programs that are covertly installed on a targeted system allowing an unauthorized user to remotely control the compromised computer for a variety of malicious purposes.
Trojan horse	A computer program that appears to have a useful function, but also has a hidden and potentially malicious function, which evades security mechanisms; for example, by masquerading as a useful program that a user likely would execute.
Virus	A computer program that can copy itself and infect a computer without the permission or knowledge of theuser. A virus might corrupt or delete data on a computer, use e-mail programs to spread to other computers, or erase everything on a hard drive. Unlike a computer worm, a virus requires human involvement (usually unwitting) to propagate.
Spamming	Sending unsolicited commercial e-mail advertising for products, services, and websites. Spam also can be used as a delivery mechanism for malware and other cyber threats.
Spoofing	Creating a fraudulent website to mimic an actual, well-known website run by another party. E-mail spoofing occurs when the sender address and other parts of an e-mail header are altered to appear as though the e-mail originated from a different source.

Source: GAO analysis of government and private-sector information security publications. | GAO-15-509.

Sources of cyber attacks can be criminal organizations and nation states (for selected other sources, see table 3). These organizations are believed to have included organized crime groups in Eastern Europe, drug cartels in Mexico, and Russian gangs. Such organizations constantly adapt to efforts to stop them, and even may have loose ties to foreign governments that help protect them. Nation-state actors are more likely to engage in cyber-espionage than to steal money from financial institutions, according to research by a major telecommunications firm. For example, they might be interested in getting information about mergers and acquisitions arranged by U.S. depository institutions for companies that compete against state-owned enterprises.

Table 3. Selected Sources of Adversarial Threats to Cybersecurity

Threat source	Description
Criminal groups	Criminal groups seek to attack systems for monetary gain. Specifically, organized criminal groups use spam, phishing, and spyware/malware to commit identity theft, online fraud, and computer extortion. International corporate spies and criminal organizations also pose a threat to the United States through their ability to conduct industrial espionage and large-scale monetary theft and to hire or develop hacker talent
Hackers	Hackers break into networks for reasons that include the thrill of the challenge, bragging rights in the hacker community, revenge, stalking, monetary gain, and political or ideological activism. While gaining unauthorized access once required a fair amount of skill or computer knowledge, hackers now can download attack scripts and protocols from the Internet and launch them against victim sites. Thus, while attack tools have become more sophisticated, they also have become easier to use. According to the Central Intelligence Agency, the large majority of hackers do not have the requisite expertise to threaten difficult targets such as critical U.S. networks. Nevertheless, the worldwide population of hackers poses a relatively high threat of an isolated or brief disruption causing serious damage.
Nation states	Nations use cyber tools as part of their information-gathering and espionage activities. In addition, several nations are aggressively working to develop information warfare doctrine, programs, and capabilities. Such capabilities enable a single entity to have a significant and serious impact by disrupting the supply, communications, and economic infrastructures that support military power—impacts that could affect the daily lives of citizens across the country. In his February 2015 testimony, the Director of National Intelligence statedthat, among state actors, China, Russia, Iran, and North Korea are of particular concern.
Insiders	The disgruntled organization insider is a principal source of computer crime. Insiders may not need a great deal of IT knowledge because their position often allows them to gain unrestricted access to cause damage tothe system or to steal system data. The insider threat includes contractors hired by the organization, as well as careless or poorly trained employees who may inadvertently introduce malware into systems.

Table 3. (Continued)

Threat source	Description
Terrorists	Terrorists seek to destroy, incapacitate, or exploit critical infrastructures to threaten national security, cause mass casualties, weaken the economy, and damage public morale and confidence. Terrorists may use phishing schemes or spyware/malware to generate funds or gather sensitive information.

Source: GAO analysis of government and private-sector information security publications. | GAO-15-509.

CYBER ATTACKS HAVE CHALLENGED DEPOSITORY INSTITUTIONS

Based on information we reviewed from federal and industry sources, depository institutions have experienced various types of cyber attacks in recent years (as noted in the following examples).

- From fall 2012 through winter 2013, several major U.S. depository institutions were subjected to distributed denial-of-service (DDOS) attacks by a hacktivist group in the Middle East, according to media reports. According to Financial Services Information Sharing and Analysis Center (FS-ISAC) staff, in some cases, access to online banking functions was interrupted for brief periods but no customer information, customer assets, or operational functions of the institutions were seriously affected.[13]
- A major U.S. depository institution suffered a data breach during summer 2014. According to public statements made by the institution, the breach compromised some account information for 83 million households and small businesses.[14] The institution maintained that no customer funds were taken, but the perpetrators obtained customer e-mail addresses, home addresses, and telephone numbers.
- U.S. depository institutions and their customers also have experienced losses through attacks known as account takeovers (see fig. 1). Based on our analysis of court documents and government issuances, these attacks typically occur when customers unknowingly install malware on their computers after receiving a phishing e-mail.

After learning of the customers' banking credentials through transmissions from the malware, the perpetrators then use the credentials to remove funds from the customers' accounts. For example, in February 2015, FBI and the Department of State announced a $3 million reward for information leading to the arrest of a Russian accused of executing account takeovers that stole more than $100 million from American bank accounts. In another example, according to a federal appeals court opinion, unknown third parties made a series of unauthorized withdrawals totaling more than $588,000 from a construction company's commercial bank account in 2009.[15] As summarized in the opinion, the unknown parties withdrew the money using the stolen online banking credentials of one of the construction company's employees including the employee identification, password, and answers to challenge questions. The withdrawals were directed to the accounts of several unknown individuals. Although the depository institution's security system assigned a high-risk score to the transactions, indicating a high probability of fraud, the construction company was not notified about the suspicious withdrawals and bank personnel did not manually review the transactions. The court, citing bank regulators' guidance, found that that the bank's security procedures for online banking were not "commercially reasonable" and reversed a lower court's ruling in favor of the bank. The appeals court required further proceedings to determine the parties' liabilities.

- ATM "skimming" also has been a growing criminal activity that cost U.S. depository institutions hundreds of millions of dollars annually, according to an FBI alert issued in July 2011. Skimming involves placing an electronic device on an ATM to retrieve information from a bank card's magnetic strip whenever a customer uses the machine. According to this alert, in fall 2010, two brothers from Bulgaria installed surreptitious surveillance equipment on New York City ATMs that allowed them to record customers' account information and personal identification numbers, create their own bank cards, and steal from customer accounts. According to the investigators, this scheme allowed the perpetrators to use the stolen information to defraud two banks of more than $1 million.

Source: GAO (adapted from *Fraud Advisory for Businesses: Corporate Account Take Over,* a joint product of the United States Secret Service, the Federal Bureau of Investigation, the Internet Crime Complaint Center, and the Financial Services Information Sharing and Analysis Center). | GAO 15-509.

Figure 1. Steps Involved in Financial Account Takeovers.

- Attacks against depository institutions in other countries also illustrate threats that U.S. depository institutions can face. For instance, the American Bankers Association testified that attacks against South Korean banks in March 2013, purportedly by persons in North Korea, shut down ATM systems for several hours and disabled more than 3,000 computers. Starting in late 2012, DOJ reported that cyber criminals penetrated the network of an India-based credit card processor for a depository institution in the United Arab Emirates, and coordinated a series of ATM withdrawals across the globe. The attack resulted in about 40,000 fraudulent ATM transactions and about $45 million in losses to the India-based credit card processor and the United Arab Emirates-based institution.

While depository institutions can face many different threat actors including nation-states, some information security vendors indicated criminal organizations perpetrated most cyber attacks against depository institutions Vendors we interviewed also indicated that large depository institutions were more likely to be targeted by nation-states and hacktivists, while smaller institutions were more commonly targeted by organized crime. For example individuals claiming to be hacktivists in Iran subjected large depository institutions to DDOS attacks during 2012 and 2013. An information security vendor we interviewed stated that criminals target smaller institutions because the expected payoff is greater relative to larger institutions whose systems are generally more sophisticated and harder to compromise. Another vendor claimed that account takeovers largely have shifted from large to medium and small institutions.

Institutions Use Multiple Methods to Help Reduce Vulnerability to Attacks but Face a Number of Challenges

Depository institutions appear to employ several methods to help reduce their vulnerability to attacks based on the size and complexity of their IT operations. On the basis of our review of 15 examinations done by bank regulators, regulatory data, and our interviews with these regulators, information security vendors, and industry associations, we found that institutions use a number of efforts to prevent intrusions and damage from cyber attacks.

- Depository institutions use access control and segregation of duties policies and procedures to limit employee access to systems that store confidential information, and control use of personal devices on their networks to help reduce the risk of cyber attacks.
- Depository institutions generally require information security training for employees to help reduce the risk from cyber threats.
- Large depository institutions may employ several employees who work full time to mitigate cyber risk, while smaller depository institutions may hire technology service providers skilled in cyber protection.
- Large institutions may have an internal audit function as well as an external auditor, while smaller institutions may rely on an external auditor only to assess their IT security.
- Institutions develop vendor management policies to oversee technology service providers.
- Institutions develop business continuity and disaster preparedness programs.
- Financial institutions must follow the Interagency Guidelines Establishing Information Security Standards.[16]

Some institutions also provide information to customers to reduce the likelihood that cyber-related problems will affect their accounts. Staff from an information security consulting firm we interviewed told us that the institutions with which their organization interacts often rated limited customer awareness of cyber risks as a key challenge. We reviewed information collected from five large depository institutions that we randomly selected from a list of large institutions generated from SNL Financial, a financial data and analysis company.[17] Our review of the five institutions' websites indicated that they generally had information intended to assist customers in taking actions to protect against phishing and malware and often provided indicators of potential fraudulent activity directed at customers' accounts. The institutions also typically described the steps they were taking to protect data, and provided customers with contact information to discuss information security concerns.

Despite these efforts, depository institutions face a number of information security challenges, according to information security vendors and federal officials we interviewed. Several information security vendors stated that institutions may not make information security a priority until they experience an incident. Other vendors and a federal official stated that institutions with more in-house IT staff generally are better able to protect themselves from attacks because they have the necessary tools, expertise, and knowledge of threat indicators. Another vendor noted that the lack of a "dedicated IT security person" can be a major concern for community banks, which generally are small institutions. He stated that, in some instances, the individual responsible for information security may have many other roles in the institution and may not have the training or sophistication required to perform such tasks as statistical analysis of data logs to detect an intrusion. However, institutions may rely on their technology service providers to conduct this type of analysis.

Some information security vendors cited specific examples of information security challenges facing depository institutions. One vendor we interviewed stated that cyber attacks will continue to worsen as mobile banking continues to grow and substantial resources would be required to keep up with changing technology, products, and vendors. A consulting firm stated that some institutions have been challenged to balance the greater efficiency of mobile devices and applications with new kinds of cyber risks. However, a 2015 report by a major telecommunications firm found that the extent to which mobile devices were infected with significant malware was low. Another vendor stated one of the greatest vulnerabilities of depository institutions was the inability to identify breaches in a timely fashion. He said that, according to his firm's research, the lag time between data breach and discovery was 9[illegible] days, and only 26 percent of attacks were identified by the affected institutions. He attributed the lag time to institutions lacking IT resources, security technology, and expertise. A report by a major telecommunications company found that in 2013 only 21 percent of successful cyber attacks against financial companies were discovered within 1 day. But a recent update of that report found that in 2014, financial institution breaches generally were detected and addressed more quickly than those in other sectors.

The Costs of Cyber Attacks Are Not Always Quantifiable

Information that specifically identifies losses by U.S. depository institutions from cyber attacks was limited. Various sources provided some estimates. For example, a large accounting firm reported that U.S. financial services companies lost more than $23 million on average from cybersecurity breaches in 2013, an increase from $16 million in 2012. An information security research firm reported that the per capita cost of data breaches in the financial industry was $206 in 2013, well above the average per capita cost of $145 for data breaches in all industries.[18]

However, identifying actual losses arising from cyber attacks can be difficult. The Center for Strategic and International Studies, a nonprofit organization, noted a number of difficulties associated with such estimates. Companies may not report their losses, may not be fully aware of what was lost, or in some cases, the losses may be difficult to estimate (for example, incidents involving the theft of details of financial transactions or mergers and acquisitions on which institutions may be advising).[19] Some estimates relied on surveys, which provide imprecise results unless carefully crafted. A survey of financial sector participants by the SANS Institute, which provides information security training and professional certifications, found that close to 80 percent of respondents could not quantify losses from attacks or did not know if their organizations could quantify them.[20]

Depository institutions also can experience costs even when the cyber incident affects an entity with which they may have no financial relationship, such as a retailer. In late 2013, cyber criminals infiltrated the point-of-sale system of the large retailer Target and stole payment card data for about 40 million customers and additional personal information of up to 70 million customers. Another U.S. retailer, Neiman Marcus, suffered a data breach that potentially exposed more than 1 million payment card accounts. Similar breaches occurred at other retailers, including Michael's Stores and Home Depot. Depository institutions incur costs from these breaches if they have to reimburse customers for unauthorized transactions that result when thieves use the card information to make purchases. After depository institutions reimburse customers for any fraudulent transactions, they can then attempt to seek restitution from the retailer at which the transaction occurred, but they may not be remunerated in every case. Depository institutions also would incur costs if they issued replacement cards with new account numbers to any of their customers whose cards had been compromised by a breach at another merchant. According to an industry association, the cost to reissue cards can be $5 per card. In other cases, institutions may choose not to reissue cards but instead incur further internal costs by conducting additional monitoring of transactions on customer accounts. Depository institutions also incur costs associated with answering customer calls and in-person inquiries about card compromises. According to data collected from members of two industry associations, the Target breach cost community banks and credit unions more than $200 million. In addition, data collected from members of an industry association estimated that the cost to community banks from the Home Depot breach was more than $90 million.

Cyber crime also can damage customer and investor confidence and institutions' reputations. A Center for Strategic and International Studies study observed that companies suffer reduced valuations (usually in the form of lower stock prices) after public reporting of cyber attacks.[21] These losses can be significant—from 1 to 5 percent—but this study also found that stock prices for affected entities usually recovered by the next quarter.[22] Also, customer deposits are a primary funding source for depository institutions, so maintaining public confidence in the institution is essential because withdrawals of significant amounts of deposits could threaten the financial soundness of the institution. An information security vendor we interviewed noted that community banks can face significant reputational risks from cyber attacks because such institutions generally rely more heavily on customer deposits as their primary funding source. At the same time, large institutions can face significant reputational risks due to greater market presence, intense media coverage, and increased reliance on capital markets.

Moreover, cyber crime can increase costs at depository institutions due to spending on additional information security to mitigate threats. Investment in information security at depository institutions has been growing as threats have increased. In October 2014, the Chairman and Chief Executive of a major U.S. depository institution stated that the institution intended to double its $250 million annual computer security budget in the next 5 years. Furthermore, some depository institutions have purchased cyber insurance to protect themselves from monetary losses. According to the Insurance Information Institute, more companies have been purchasing cyber coverage. 23 According to this institute, premiums on such policies can range from a few thousand dollars for base coverage for small businesses (less than $10 million in revenue) to several hundred thousand dollars for major corporations desiring comprehensive coverage.

Regulators Use a Risk-based Approach to Overseeing Information Security That Could Benefit from Additional Data Analysis

Regulators oversee the adequacy of information security at depository institutions using a risk-based examination approach and have guidance that incorporates best practices. The regulators assess an institution's risk level and determine appropriate examination procedures by reviewing risk assessments, results of past examinations, and any IT changes. Effectively examining more highly complex IT environments requires staff with specialized IT expertise; regulators have been taking steps to hire more IT examiners and provide IT training to existing examiners. The regulators collected and analyzed some limited information from IT examinations, but were not routinely aggregating and analyzing data on deficiencies found in individual examinations. Cyber risks affecting a depository institution can arise from weaknesses in practices of technology service providers; therefore, FDIC, the Federal Reserve, and OCC also conduct examinations of providers' information security. However, as discussed in detail below, NCUA lacks the authority to examine these third-party service providers.

Regulator Guidance on Information Security Incorporates Leading Practices

The four bank regulators have issued guidance that addresses risk-focused examinations and incorporates best practices for information security. The guidance describes the processes examiners should follow for risk-focused supervision—in which examiners identify and then focus on the areas that pose the highest risk to institutions. These processes include conducting and validating risk assessments to help scope the examinations. For example, the Federal Reserve's manual for conducting examinations of commercial banks directs examiners in preparing the risk assessment to take into account the quality of the institution's own management processes, but states that testing should be sufficient to fully assess the degree of risk exposure in a particular function or activity. FDIC's Manual of Examination Policies says that examiners should consider the adequacy of audit and control practices when determining a bank's risk profile and, when appropriate, try to reduce regulatory burdens by testing rather than duplicating the work of a bank's audit and control functions. NCUA's Examiner Guide directs its examiners to use a risk-focused program to evaluate the degree to which credit union management identifies, measures, monitors, and controls the existing potential risks in their operations.

The guidance regulators used to assess institutions' information security practices conformed to leading practices that are recommended for federal agencies. The regulators have been examining depository institutions for information technology since 1978. In 1980, the regulators working through the Federal Financial Institutions Examination Council (FFIEC) first published IT examination guidance. In 2001, the regulators separated the guidance into separate booklets. The Information Technology Examination Handbook currently comprises 11 booklets addressing topics such as electronic banking, information security, and outsourcing technology services.[24] In our December 2011 report on critical infrastructure protection, we reviewed the handbook and compared it with federal IT guidelines. We found the handbook incorporated 196 of the 198 security practices recommended by the federal IT guidelines at that time.[25] The bank regulators have continued to update the FFIEC handbook and issue additional joint and agency guidance. Specifically, FFIEC officials said they made changes in response to the cybersecurity framework that the National Institute of Standards and Technology issued.[26] Additionally, the Gramm-LeachBliley Act in 1999 mandated that the regulators issue information security standards for financial institutions to safeguard sensitive customer information.[27] In response, the regulators issued interagency guidelines in 2001.[28] They also have issued guidance requiring financial institutions to develop programs for responding to instances in which unauthorized access to customer information has occurred.[29]

In addition to the FFIEC handbook, the regulators have jointly or separately issued guidance to address various specific security threats that depository institutions have recently experienced, including DDOS attacks, corporate account takeovers, malware/advanced persistent threats, ATM vulnerabilities, and credit/debit card breaches. For example, FFIEC issued a joint statement on mitigating DDOS attacks, and depository institutions are expected to take the appropriate steps as part of their business continuity, incident response, and disaster recovery plans to address the potential of a DDOS attack.[30] The FFIEC also issued joint guidance in April 2014 on how institutions should address a recently discovered significant vulnerability that threatened to expose encrypted information.[31] See appendix II for a list of cybersecurity guidance applicable to the banking and finance sector.

Regulators Examine Information Security Based on Assessments of the Risks at Individual Institutions

In accordance with their risk-focused approach, regulators conduct a risk assessment for an institution's IT functions to help determine the scope of an IT examination.[32] The regulators' examination authority states that they must ensure that operational risks, including those arising from cyber incidents, do not harm an institution's safety and soundness.[33] Examiners use information provided by the institution, a review of past examination results, and a review of any IT changes that took place at the institution since the last examination. Additionally, each of the regulators expects its examiners to develop a solid understanding of the IT systems of the institution they plan to examine, regardless of the institution's size. The risk assessments generally include technical information about the systems and how these systems relate to the institution's business lines. Regulators told us that during the examination, examiners assess both internal and external risk for the institutions. For example, FDIC uses a tool called the IT Officer's Questionnaire that asks examiners to assess the institution's safeguards and protections against internal and external threats and vulnerabilities to confidential customer information; the likelihood and impact of identified threats and vulnerabilities; and the sufficiency of policies, procedures, and customer information to control risks. In addition, FDIC's Technology Supervision Branch assesses cybersecurity risks and shares that information with examiners. OCC officials told us that to help better assess external threats to depository institutions, they have formed an internal working group to coordinate with other government agencies, industry groups, and other organizations to monitor outside threats, and information obtained from this group is used to inform examination strategies. Similarly, in June 2013, FFIEC created a Cybersecurity and Critical Infrastructure Working Group to coordinate the sharing of external threat information across its member agencies.[34]

When determining the scope of the review at individual institutions, the regulators told us their examiners also consider how much information is to be sought and reviewed, and what level of IT proficiency the assigned examiners will need to conduct the examination. For example, FDIC staff said when an institution is determined to be low risk, has not had any changes in its IT since the last examination, and received a high rating for its IT functions in the previous examination, its examiners may not review all IT-related areas in the current examination cycle. Regulators also told us that the IT programs of some smaller institutions often were not complex enough to warrant reviews against all the elements of the FFIEC or agency guidance; thus, they omitted those elements from the examination. Alternatively, if an institution was deemed to be higher risk, such as by having more complex IT systems or conducting considerable activities over the Internet or other electronic networks, examiners might choose to assess it against more of the elements of the applicable guidance to ensure the institution had been adequately securing its IT systems.

On the basis of our review of examination materials of 15 banks and credit unions conducted in 2013, we found that bank regulators undertook various activities to assess the adequacy of institutions' information security practices.[35] In the 15 sets of examination materials we reviewed, examiners used relevant parts of their guidance depending on what issues they were attempting to examine. We noted they reviewed documentation such as risk assessments conducted by the institutions, internal and external IT audit results and IT audit management functions, disaster recovery and business continuity plans for continuing computer operations (including after cyber attacks), and vendor management oversight. In one examination, examiners reviewed an external audit report that looked at several areas.[36]

Ensuring Adequate Staff with IT Expertise Poses Challenges

As IT use and the sophistication IT usage increases, the regulators acknowledged that hiring and training sufficient numbers of staff with the expertise needed to conduct detailed examinations of information security systems could be challenging. According to information the regulators provided us, each agency employs staff with advanced IT expertise. The regulators are responsible for examining thousands of depository institutions, and as of early 2015, reported the following:

- FDIC, which is the primary regulator for more than 4,000 institutions, had 60 premium IT examiners who are highly skilled in conducting IT examinations. These staff are primarily used in examinations of institutions with highly complex IT infrastructure.[37] Additionally, FDIC has 32 IT examination analysts and more than 100 subject-matter experts who assist in reviews at other institutions.[38]
- OCC, the primary regulator for more than 1,500 banks and thrifts had 100 dedicated IT specialist examiners, with more than 40 assigned to reviews of its 19 largest banks.[39] Another 48 of the IT specialist examiners were distributed among OCC's four districts to assist with examinations of medium and complex institutions. Some staff were also part of an IT policy group that focuses on drafting and maintaining OCC and FFIEC IT supervisory guidance. Additionally,

OCC general safety and soundness examiners who have received IT training conduct examinations of IT issues at some institutions.

- NCUA, which regulates more than 6,200 credit unions, had 40 to 50 subject-matter IT examiners, as well as 12 IT specialists in regional offices and 4 in headquarters. These staff focus primarily on the largest credit unions, but regular examiner staff consult with the specialists on IT issues that arise at reviews of other institutions.
- Federal Reserve, which regulates more than 5,500 institutions, had more than 85 IT examiners who have information security or advanced IT expertise and focus primarily on examinations of the largest institutions.

As a result of the numbers of staff with IT expertise at each agency, the regulators generally have not used IT experts during the examinations of medium and small institutions, which are often determined to be low risk. According to regulators, IT and information security examinations at low-risk institutions are typically conducted by generalists trained in IT rather than specialists because the specialists are usually used only on the higher-risk examinations. According to the regulators, they may have several IT vendors on-site at the large institutions with complex IT programs. However, regulators may assign a generalist examiner with some IT training to conduct examinations at medium and small banks.[40] For example, OCC, which is the regulator for some of the largest institutions, may send about 15 IT examiners to conduct an IT examination at a large institution, but may have only 1 IT examiner for several medium and small institutions. FDIC officials said when determining what level of examiner to send to an institution, they consider the institution's technology profile. For the most-complex institutions and technology service providers, they will deploy premium-grade IT examiners and subject-matter vendors. FDIC also uses non-examiner IT examination analysts (who have specialized IT skills but are not qualified to serve as examiner-in-charge) to assist examiners with IT examinations, including the least-complex institutions.

Having additional staff with specific IT expertise can help the regulators conduct reviews that prove even more useful to institutions. For example, one institution we interviewed also noted the benefits of having examiners with specific IT and information security expertise conduct reviews. Representatives of this medium-sized depository institution told us that they received an in-depth IT examination from FDIC a few years ago that their staff found useful. The examiner who conducted the review recommended a number of system advances that the institution's staff told us were expensive to implement, but improved cybersecurity performance. However, staff said that the regular examiners performed the subsequent examinations, which were not as specific and useful as the review that involved the examiner with IT expertise.

Regulators have been seeking to improve their information security oversight and have discussed efforts to expand the numbers of staff with IT and information security expertise. For example, since January 2010, FDIC has had ongoing training efforts to increase IT knowledge. Every examiner commissioned since that time must complete four courses that provide a baseline education for IT within 2 years of their commission date. As of December 2014, FDIC reported that 25 percent of examiners had completed all four courses and 75 percent completed between one and three courses. FDIC also increased the number of IT examination analysts and subject-matter experts in the past few years. Other regulators plan to add more IT examiners as well. OCC stated that it has plans to hire additional examiners with the knowledge and experience to effectively assess the complex products and systems being implemented in depository institutions. NCUA plans to offer a web-based course to train safety and soundness examiners for IT and Federal Reserve officials stated that they plan some increase in IT staff expertise, but have been seeking to repurpose existing resources first.

In addition, as the result of a recent, special, large-scale review of about 500 community financial institutions, the regulators have identified various efforts to improve their activities, including conducting more training for their staff and updating their guidance. In the summer of 2014, staff from the four regulators conducted a special pilot cybersecurity assessment at institutions under the auspices of FFIEC in recognition of the growing importance of the need for effective information security for such institutions. The assessment was done in conjunction with normally scheduled examinations of about 500 community financial institutions. FFIEC officials told us that the questions examiners asked during these examinations were primarily process-oriented, and included questions about metrics and scorecards. Following this assessment, FFIEC provided depository institutions with a list of questions they could ask internally to assess their preparedness to deal with cyber threats. Recently, FFIEC officials issued a press release announcing several changes they plan to make as a result of the assessment. These include issuing a self-assessment tool to use to evaluate their inherent cybersecurity risks and preparedness; developing additional training programs for regulator staff on evolving cyber threats and vulnerabilities; and updating the IT Examination

Handbook to reflect evolving cyber threats and vulnerabilities.[41] Additionally, the Federal Reserve Bank of New York recently announced that it formed a team to reassess its framework for cybersecurity assessment and establish a new risk-based approach for its state member banks. The team has been working in coordination with the Board of Governors.

Additional Analysis Could Help Regulators Better Assess Risk While Scoping IT Examinations

Regulators were not routinely collecting and aggregating data on IT deficiencies in formats that would allow them to analyze trends that could improve examinations at other institutions. Although each regulator described collecting some information across examinations to assist its oversight, the regulators did not have standardized methods for collecting examination data that could allow them to readily analyze trends in specific information security problems across institutions. In response to our request for information on the number of deficiencies identified during examinations that included information systems and technology, the information that regulators provided varied in detail and generally was not broken into categories that differentiated the types of deficiencies found. Federal internal control standards provide that management should have relevant, reliable, and timely information on key agency activities.[42] These standards state that key information on an entity's operations should be recorded and communicated to management and others within the entity and within a time frame that enables management to carry out its internal control and other responsibilities. Regulators explained that in some cases, their different reporting systems made consistent collection difficult or procedures did not address systematic collection of such data. OCC staff said that compiling such information was more difficult because they use different systems to track deficiencies at larger banks than they use for medium and smaller institutions. On a quarterly basis, FDIC manually reviews all IT examination reports and compiles information on deficiencies at individual institutions generally only when the deficiency causes a downgrade in the rating of the quality of the institution's practices, but such data are not tracked for institutions that are rated satisfactory or better.[43]

The regulators also varied in the extent to which they could provide data on actual incidents at their regulated institutions. Under interagency guidance, institutions' response programs must contain procedures to notify their regulator when they have reason to believe that a data breach occurred that compromised sensitive customer information.[44] FDIC reported that it collects and analyzes information on all data breaches reported by its supervised financial institutions, as well as other security incidents identified during examinations. NCUA does not maintain a centralized database on data breach reports—each region holds the data—but periodically reviews incident reports and has been working to expand its analytic capabilities in this area. OCC reported that all national banks and federal savings associations are expected to report to OCC as soon as possible after they become aware of an incident involving unauthorized access to or use of sensitive customer information. OCC officials said that its local supervisory offices maintain this information. The Federal Reserve said that its staff enter IT incident information into a customized application when notified of an incident. However, the data that the regulators collected on these incidences were not centrally compiled and analyzed.

Compiling such data and analyzing it more broadly has proven beneficial in other areas. We noted in a January 2000 report that neither the Federal Reserve nor OCC collect aggregated information on the risks that examiners identified during examinations. We concluded that such aggregation might have proven useful in the Long Term Capital Management hedge fund case—although regulators had identified individual credit exposures that numerous banks had to this fund, the potential for the fund to disrupt markets was not realized until after the fund's near collapse.[45] Similarly, in a February 2009 report, we found that bank regulators' oversight of institutions' anti-money-laundering activities could be improved by aggregating information about deficiencies.[46] Without collecting and analyzing data more consistently, regulators have not obtained information that could identify broader IT issues affecting their regulated entities, and better target their IT risk assessments.

Although Other Regulators Examine Technology Service Providers Used by Their Institutions, NCUA Lacks Such Authority

Unlike the bank regulators, NCUA lacks authority to examine third-party service providers, such as technology service providers, on which credit unions often rely to perform critical functions. As we previously found in an October 2003 report, these third-party arrangements can help credit unions manage costs, provide expertise, and improve services to members, but they also present risks, such as threats to security systems, weakness of products, availability and integrity of systems, and confidentiality of information.[47] When relying on third-party providers, credit unions subject themselves to operational and reputational risks if they do not manage these providers appropriately. In addition, managing the providers can be difficult because smaller institutions may lack leverage in their contractual relationships to obtain information to help them determine whether providers have been performing adequately.

Under the Bank Service Company Act, FDIC, the Federal Reserve, and OCC have the authority to supervise and examine third-party service providers such as technology service providers.[48] Similarly, under the Consumer Financial Protection Act of 2010, the Bureau of Consumer Financial Protection has supervisory authority over service providers to which supervised banks and nonbanks outsourced services.[49] However, the Federal Credit Union Act does not grant similar authority to NCUA, and has not been amended to grant NCUA permanent authority to examine technology service providers (NCUA had temporary authority to examine technology service providers for Y2K purposes).[50] NCUA officials told us that their agency has sought such authority for about a decade, but such authority has not been granted.

According to the other regulators, their examinations of the technology service providers (that conduct sufficient activities for depository institutions to warrant a review) follow a format similar to that for the depository institution examinations. These providers are also rated using the same measures used for depository institutions. FDIC, the Federal Reserve, and OCC often conduct the examinations jointly, with one regulator serving as the lead agency. Following the examination, the reports of examination are sent to the depository institutions that contract with the technology service provider usually only if the provider receives low ratings for its IT practices. This is intended to help depository institutions manage their vendors and inform them of potential risks that may exist with any of the IT services they obtain from these providers. Service providers that are found deficient in a particular area generally would receive notice of required actions necessary to remedy the deficiency as would a depository institution, and the regulators would follow up to ensure that actions were taken in the appropriate time frame.[51]

In contrast, because NCUA lacks similar authority to conduct direct examinations of technology service providers that conduct processing for credit unions, that agency uses other means to monitor and reduce risks to credit unions arising from technology service providers. These include making requests to the provider that it submit to a voluntary examination, but NCUA staff noted that some providers offering services exclusively to credit union clients have rejected NCUA voluntary examinations. NCUA staff also attempt to assess service providers by participating in examinations of providers conducted by the other bank regulators, but the other regulators do not always allow them to participate. NCUA directs credit unions to take steps to ensure that the technology service providers they use address observed deficiencies. For instance, credit unions might end contracts with poorly-performing providers. However, without supervisory authority over these providers, NCUA cannot enforce any corrective actions and can only make recommendations and present findings to the credit unions that use those providers.

Industry associations that represent credit unions and organizations that provide third-party services to credit unions have opposed granting NCUA examination authority over third-party providers, such as technology service providers. They said that such examinations would be an unnecessary intrusion into these entities' operations because the credit unions using the providers can provide information to NCUA about providers' activities and this oversight should be adequate for the regulator. In contrast, NCUA states that its lack of authority over providers poses a regulatory burden for credit unions, because the agency must rely upon credit unions to report certain information on the providers with which they do business. Small credit unions have been particularly affected, because they must rely on third-party providers for many products and services that larger credit unions could provide in-house. NCUA stated that these credit unions could benefit from increased usage of NCUA's existing resources and expertise to review the adequacy of cybersecurity controls in place at technology service providers.

We have long supported granting NCUA such authority. In a July 1999 report, we found that joint regulatory examinations of third-party service providers might increase the economy and efficiency of federal oversight of Internet banking activities. At the time, NCUA's temporary authority to examine third-party providers was set to expire in December 2001. We suggested that Congress consider extending NCUA's temporary examination authority beyond 2001.[52] The authority was not extended. In an October 2003 report, we found that NCUA had adopted a risk focused examination program but faced challenges in implementing it, partly because NCUA lacked authority to examine third-party service providers, on which credit unions increasingly relied to provide services.[53] We asked that Congress consider granting NCUA legislative authority to examine third-party service providers that provide services to credit unions and are not examined through the other federal banking agencies. This matter was never implemented.[54] We maintain that NCUA would benefit from this authority. The services of the third-party providers are integral to the operations of many credit unions, and deficiencies in providers' operations quickly could become deficiencies that produce financial and other harm at credit unions. In its response to our 2003 report, NCUA also stated that because many third-party service providers service numerous credit unions, a failure of a provider posed systemic risk issues. In its 2015 annual report, FSOC calls for granting NCUA examination and enforcement authority over third-party service providers in an effort to close what FSOC describes as a significant regulatory gap. We agree with this assessment. Without authority to examine third-party service providers, NCUA risks not being able to effectively monitor the safety and soundness of regulated credit unions.

DEPOSITORY INSTITUTIONS FACE CHALLENGES OBTAINING CYBER THREAT INFORMATION, BUT TREASURY AND OTHERS HAVE BEEN TAKING STEPS TO IMPROVE INFORMATION SHARING

Numerous entities, including public-private partnerships, media, technology service providers, federal agencies, and other depository institutions, are sources of threat information to financial institutions, including depository institutions, and efforts are under way to develop better mechanisms to share this information. FS-ISAC is a central resource for cyber threat information for institutions in the financial sector. FS-ISAC is one of a number of centers that were established within industry sectors identified as having critical infrastructure in response to Presidential Decision Directive 63 (issued in 1998).[55] Within these centers, security specialists identify, analyze, and share information; collaborate on threats, incidents, vulnerabilities, and best practices; and work to protect their respective industries from cyber and physical threats. These centers also can provide risk mitigation and alerts. Some centers have permanent staff, while others rely on volunteer personnel from companies within their respective sector.

FS-ISAC was started in 1999 as a member-owned nonprofit that entered into partnerships with other industry groups, associations, and government agencies.

It has broad industry representation, with more than 5,000 members worldwide, and has 30 permanent staff working full-time on threat analysis and information sharing. When FS-ISAC learns of an attack or has other relevant information to share with the sector, it follows a "traffic light" protocol in which alerts are color coded to indicate who can access the information.

The alert color is controlled by the originator of the message and works as follows:

- Red— restricted to a defined group (e.g., only those present in a meeting).
- Amber—information is restricted to FS-ISAC members.
- Green—information can be shared with FS-ISAC members and partners (e.g., DHS, Treasury, and other government agencies and ISACs), but is not to be shared with public forums.
- White—publicly available information subject to copyright rules.[56]

FS-ISAC also removes identifying data from all of this information so that breached institutions remain anonymous, thereby helping to protect the institutions' reputations. Finally, FS-ISAC recently deployed an automated system for disseminating alerts to member institutions with the goal of giving potential victims a fuller picture of the threat using standardized language. This system, called Soltra Edge, was developed in conjunction with DHS, which funded open specifications for automated threat information sharing, and the Depository Trust and Clearing Corporation.[57] FS-ISAC told us that a number of large financial institutions are early adopters of this technology. According to an industry association official, FS-ISAC has been a key resource on cyber threats for the financial sector and has built a high level of trust over the years.

In addition to this center, financial institutions, including depository institutions, obtain considerable information about cyber threats from publicly available media, security experts, and technology service providers. Internet sources, such as blogs, media reports, rich site summary feeds, and bulletin boards provide information about cybersecurity events and threats. 58 Technology service providers also can offer a unique perspective on information security because they provide IT services to several institutions and sometimes to several industries.

Depository institutions also receive cyber threat information from Treasury. Treasury's Office of Critical Infrastructure Protection and Compliance Policy (OCIP) facilitates sharing of information among financial institutions and between the public and private sectors, among other things. Within OCIP, Treasury's Financial Sector Cyber Intelligence Group was created in 2013. It monitors and analyzes intelligence, including from the intelligence community, on cyber threats to the financial sector and provides the threat information to the sector. Its purpose is to increase the volume, timeliness, and quality of cyber threat information shared between the government and the financial services sector. The group produces threat and vulnerability circulars for financial institutions that are released through FS-ISAC, DHS's Homeland Security Information Network Financial Services portal, and an e-mail list that includes financial regulators and trade associations. Since April 2013, this group has released 36 circulars. Treasury officials told us that the amount of detail in these circulars varies depending on the information being shared. For instance, one circular focused on identified common vulnerabilities and exposures because the group received reports that certain threat actors were preparing to use the vulnerabilities to target critical infrastructure. In addition, the group released information about various Internet protocol addresses associated with malware or threat actors and, when applicable, included steps that institutions could take (such as contacting FBI) if a particular address appeared in their network. We examined two recent issuances by the group, and found that each provided a description of certain advanced persistent threats to the financial sector and information to help detect and mitigate them.

The Cyber Intelligence Group also responds to requests for information from employees of financial institutions and FS-ISAC about suspicious activity on their networks. The group told us that it facilitates the sharing of classified information through classified briefings to financial regulators that are members of FBIIC and cleared members and employees of FSISAC and financial institutions. The group also participates in general discussions and ad hoc meetings and briefings with individual financial institutions. In addition, Treasury staff told us that FS-ISAC has a formal process for requesting information anonymously from Treasury using sanitized submissions from financial institutions. Staff from the Cyber Intelligence Group told us they attempt to respond to these requests within 1 to 5 days, depending on the priority specified by FS-ISAC. Treasury told us that it handled 46 formal requests from FS-ISAC from January 2014 to April 2015.

DHS also can be a significant source of the cyber threat information for depository institutions. DHS is the primary civilian agency responsible for sharing cyber threat information with critical infrastructure sectors, including depository institutions. DHS maintains a Protected Critical Infrastructure Information program to protect information voluntarily shared by the private sector with DHS to be used for homeland security purposes.

- Within DHS, the NCCIC is a 24-hour cyber situational awareness, incident response, and management center for federal cybersecurity. In the center, staff from various federal agencies with intelligence, law enforcement, and critical infrastructure protection missions are able to monitor cyber incidents and share information with the private sector to provide greater understanding of cybersecurity vulnerabilities, intrusions, incidents, mitigation, and recovery actions.[59] The United States Computer Emergency Readiness Team is the 24-hour operational arm of the integration center. To assist the financial sector, staff from Treasury and FS-ISAC are also present at this center to ensure that information that could increase readiness and improve protections is provided to depository institutions and other financial sector entities.
- DHS set up the Cyber Information Sharing and Collaboration Program to collaborate with owners and operators of critical infrastructure and leverage government and industry subject-matter expertise to respond to cybersecurity incidents. DHS staff told us that the program has monthly and quarterly meetings (classified and unclassified) that include senior government officials and management of private-sector institutions. This program also conducts advanced technical exchange meetings that cover emerging threats. FS-ISAC representatives participate in these meetings.
- DHS told us that it also has developed outreach programs to assist critical infrastructure sectors to prepare for cyber attacks. For instance, DHS offers Cyber Resilience Reviews, which are no-cost, voluntary, nontechnical assessments that evaluate an organization's operational resilience and cybersecurity practices. According to DHS, it has conducted such reviews of 18 firms in the financial services sector, including some large and medium-sized banks, since 2010.

Financial institutions, including depository institutions, also receive information from law enforcement agencies that collect cyber threat information through investigations. Law enforcement organizations can notify an institution directly if they possess information pertaining specifically to the institution. They share general declassified threat information with the relevant critical infrastructure sectors.

- The National Cyber Investigative Joint Task Force was established in 2008 by presidential directive to be the focal point for all government agencies to coordinate, integrate, and share information related to domestic cyber threat investigations. The FBI serves as the executive agent for the task force, which includes 20 different partners such as DHS, Secret Service, Central Intelligence Agency, local law enforcement, and representatives from the U.S. military. The task force shares information obtained through investigation with institutions using FBI Liaison Alert System reports that provide trend information and technical indicators. In addition, FBI's Cyber Division shares threat information using Private Industry Notification reports that provide an overview of certain threats. These reports may be directed to specific industries, including financial services, to inform companies about past attacks and provide information to identify and defend against further attacks. Depository institutions and other financial sector participants also obtain information about emerging cyber risks through meetings in which financial sector executives are granted 1-day security clearances to hear briefings on threats and recommended mitigation steps.
- The Secret Service Electronic Crimes Task Force was started in 1995 and expanded nationwide in 2001, and is the operational entity within Secret Service that investigates cyber crime. The Cyber Intelligence section at Secret Service headquarters focuses on the financial sector and analyzes information from the task force to identify threats. The Secret Service provides information to individual institutions and FS-ISAC. Secret Service officials told us that because they work with non-classified information and focus on law enforcement, they have more freedom to share information with the private sector than the intelligence community.

See figure 2 for cyber threat information sources discussed above and additional sources referenced by financial institutions we interviewed.

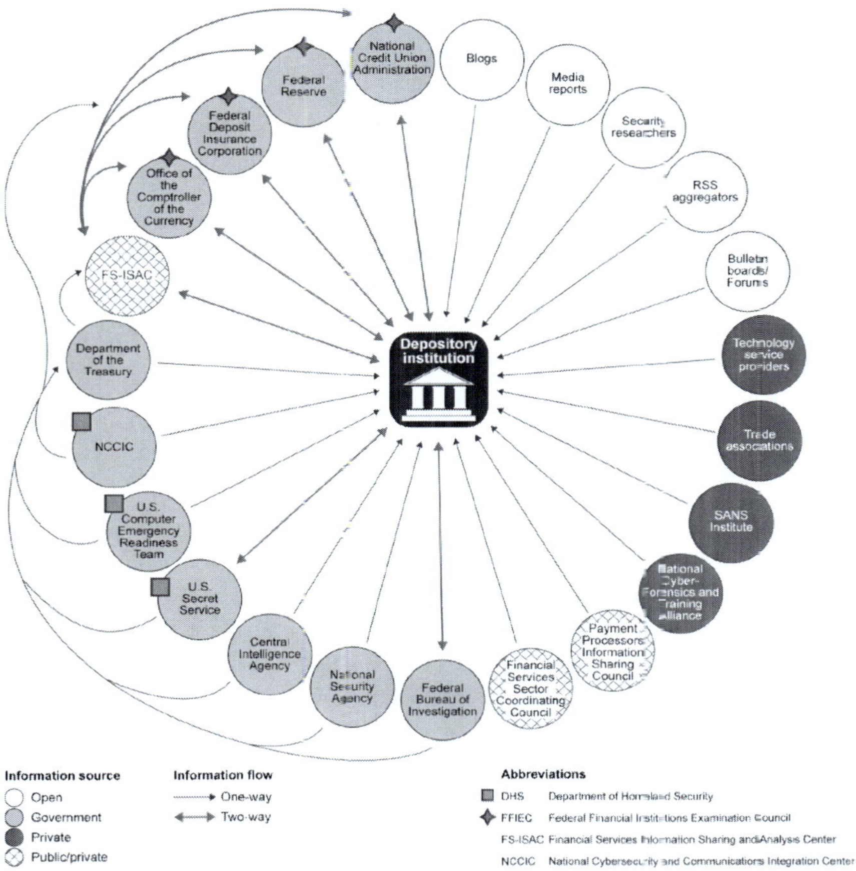

Source: GAO. | GAO-15-509.

Figure 2. Selected Sources of Cyber Threat Information, Based on GAO Interviews.

Obtaining Adequate Information on Cyber Threats Has Been Challenging

Although various federal entities attempt to provide cyber threat information to financial institutions including depository institutions, efforts are under way to respond to challenges that can limit the timeliness and quality of information that is shared. Data breaches and security incidents require rapid response to mitigate impact; therefore, effective preparation or responses require timely and useable information. A good understanding of known threats and controls can guide depository institutions to secure their systems. In several forums we held in October and November 2014 that included more than 50 depository institutions and other members of the financial sector, participants told us that information they received from government sources about cyber threats often was repetitive, not timely, and could not always be acted upon because the information lacked sufficient details.

Information from Different Sources Could Be Repetitive

Financial institutions indicated that they often received repetitive information. Representatives from institutions we interviewed stated that they rarely obtained cyber threat information from the government that they had not already received from other sources. Also, they mentioned that federal agencies repeated information during a cyber incident. For example, information might first be provided by the FBI, then the Federal Reserve, then the Secret Service, and then DHS, but most, if not all of the information, was repeated. Depository institutions assign staff to review this information to see if the various federal notices provide new information. Representatives stated that they would prefer some kind of incident numbering system or other method that would help them save time processing information.

Representatives from smaller institutions also noted that they sometimes struggled with the volume of information from different vendors and government sources. In our interviews, some representatives said that government agencies should make more effort to aggregate or categorize the information to help institutions more easily use it to better protect themselves. Some representatives noted that the United States Computer Emergency Readiness Team in DHS attempts to categorize alerts, but some other representatives stated that they would like more efforts in this area. According to Treasury officials, this is an area that they plan to address through ongoing improvement efforts.

Various Barriers Hampered Cyber Information Sharing

Institution representatives indicated that obtaining more timely information about active attacks affecting other institutions would be helpful, but various barriers hamper this sharing. Having such information allows them to better check their own systems for potential intrusions or implement protections to prevent any such events. Representatives from depository institutions we interviewed stated that obtaining information quickly was especially important when a security incident became a major media story and institutions needed information to offset inaccurate speculation about the impact of the incident.

Although information arising from a successful attack or breach at another institution could prove helpful to other institutions, information security vendors and federal officials told us that institutions under active attack often have been reluctant or might not be able to share information about the attacks in a timely manner. Under guidance established by the bank regulators as required by the Gramm-Leach-Bliley Act, institutions have various requirements to notify their regulator and consumers when they determine that the misuse of customer information occurred or was reasonably possible.[60] In addition, these institutions can be covered by other state and local laws that require government entities and private-sector firms to provide notice to customers of potential breaches of consumer information as a result of cyber or other incidents. For example, according to the National Conference of State Legislatures, as of January 2015, 47 states, three U.S. territories, and the District of Columbia had enacted standards for data breach notification.[61] Some institutions we interviewed said they were concerned about reputational damage from such disclosures, which they said reduces their willingness to share with other institutions specifics about how they were breached. In addition, some institutions said that sharing information with law enforcement can result in that information being treated as classified or investigation sensitive, which then prevents the institution from easily sharing it with other institutions that want to avoid a similar breach.

Institutions also might be unable to obtain cyber threat information because other institutions were not required or willing to share it with some government agencies because of concerns that such information could be made public later. For example, institutions told Treasury that they were sometimes reluctant to share information with the agency because the information might be publicly released under the Freedom of Information Act. Treasury may consider whether the information qualifies for an exemption from disclosure under the act, but only after the information has been submitted. They noted that DHS has authority to prevent shared information from being released under the Freedom of Information Act through its Protected Critical Infrastructure Information program, but Treasury does not have such authority. Treasury officials told us that they have been working with DHS to certify staff to access protected critical infrastructure information that would be protected from public disclosure under the DHS program.

FS-ISAC has facilitated information sharing among financial institutions. For example, during DDOS attacks in 2012 to 2013, institution representatives noted that various institutions shared contextual information about the attacks through FS-ISAC. However, some officials said that institutions were less concerned about confidentiality in this case because several institutions were subject to the same type of attack. Some representatives from institutions we interviewed expressed skepticism about the efficacy of FS-ISAC because of concerns that other institutions would use confidential information shared through FS-ISAC for competitive advantage, such as by attempting to lure away customers of institutions that experienced cyber attacks.

Information Shared Not Always Sufficiently Detailed to Be Useful

Information that is shared about cyber threats and actual attacks was not always seen as having sufficient context or details to allow depository institutions to take definitive actions to protect themselves. Representatives from institutions we interviewed expressed the need for information with sufficient detail to allow them to examine their systems and take precautions. They also noted that in many instances government agencies are unable to share such information because it is from classified sources and agencies can be reluctant to declassify the information to avoid revealing methods and sources used to obtain it. The financial institution representatives noted that what they hoped to obtain was information on how an attack would happen, rather than how the information was obtained. One representative commented that institutions did not need more people with security clearances but rather usable data that were released more quickly.

Federal officials we interviewed stated that intelligence community and law enforcement officials were cautious about declassifying certain contextual information out of concern for divulging sources and methodology used to uncover cyber threats. For instance, FBI and Secret Service staff said they have tried not to "victimize the victims" of cyber crimes through information sharing relating to ongoing investigations.

That is, a depository institution that suffered fraudulent credit and debit card transactions because of a data breach at another entity might want to know the identity of the entity to prevent further fraud and seek restitution for lost funds. DOJ has a statutory obligation to protect those who share critical infrastructure information and seeks to ensure that such information is secure.[62]

Institutions also expressed the desire to obtain detailed information. Representatives from large institutions we interviewed stated that contextual information (such as any code, pathways, or tactics associated with the attack) was not always given with threat indicators. The lack of context can be problematic because the operating environment of some institutions is complicated, so that simply supplying the Internet address from where the attack originated would not adequately assist the institutions. An institution representative told us that having additional context can allow them to better focus their information security efforts. For instance, information that included the threat vector—generally, the path or tool used to attack the target—could be more readily acted upon.[63] One representative said that receiving examples of responses to particular types of attacks (such as a list of what worked and what did not work) could be helpful. Representatives from other institutions noted that when it received indicators with context, the institution was more able to address the threats. One institution's representative said that receiving insufficiently detailed information was similar to telling the institution that it might be attacked by a criminal in a red hat. But saying that a criminal in a red hat, would go behind the building, and use a crowbar to force the door open would provide enough detail for the institution to better target its defenses. Although such detail can be helpful, Treasury officials told us that large financial institutions have told them that having incomplete threat information was still preferable to having no information. Treasury staff told us that they have continued to work with other federal agencies to obtain information that can be shared with financial institutions and has as much context as possible without compromising sources and methods used to acquire it.

Treasury Has Been Taking Steps to Improve Information Sharing

Treasury has continued to take various steps to improve the information the federal government shares with financial institutions, including depository institutions. Treasury's Cyber Intelligence Group was established to provide the financial sector with a federal focal point for improved sharing of cyber threat-related information. Through discussions with financial institutions, FSSCC, and FS-ISAC, Treasury staff have been working to determine what information the financial sector needed to better protect themselves from cyber threats. According to Treasury staff, the two main types of information that financial institutions hoped to receive were

- strategic intelligence on threat actors and their capabilities so institutions could better prioritize their resources and defenses; and

- tactical information on the targets, methods, and tools employed by threat actors, including entry methods, network entry points, and methods of access, type of access gained, names and content of malicious files, and use of open source or publicly available shared tools.

In addition to the activities of the Cyber Intelligence Group described earlier, Treasury has been working to provide such information to financial institutions by:

- disseminating cyber intelligence requirements of the financial sector to the intelligence community and law enforcement that will better enable those groups to identify specific threat information for the sector;
- seeking declassification of cyber threat indicators and analysis from the intelligence community and law enforcement for distribution by the Cyber Intelligence Group or federal partners;
- collaborating with other federal agencies to produce Joint Analysis Reports containing declassified cyber threat indicators; and
- electronically distributing circulars and Treasury Early Warning Indicator reports (which describe organized and sophisticated attempts by cyber actors to penetrate Treasury's own networks) through FS-ISAC that could assist financial institutions with implementing protections for their own systems.

In addition, Treasury prepared a guide to the Homeland Security Information Network Financial Services Portal with information on membership eligibility, and how to join the portal and setup e-mail notifications, and posted all financial sector-related cyber threat information that was federally produced to the portal.[64] Treasury staff indicated that this guide was intended to make financial institutions aware of and assist them with obtaining access to this additional source of information on cyber threats.

Treasury officials acknowledged that the intelligence community and law enforcement require a certain amount of time to collect, analyze, produce, and disseminate intelligence that is responsive to the financial sector needs. They saw this as similar to the circumstances after the September 11 attacks when establishing intelligence requirements on terrorist networks also took time. Treasury officials stated they have attempted to ensure that the information provided to institutions did not duplicate information provided by other sources by:

- participating in daily, weekly, and other periodic interagency coordination calls and information sharing working groups;
- detailing staff to other agencies to identify what already had been shared or was being prepared for dissemination;
- occasionally recommending to other agencies that certain information of use to multiple sectors be declassified and released to multiple sectors, including the financial sector;
- joining FS-ISAC and subscribing to multiple mailing lists to ascertain what other sources were distributing; and
- asking institutions to notify them if they saw the information on the Cyber Intelligence Group's circulars elsewhere.

Treasury officials stated that they rarely heard from institutions that the circulars duplicated other notices.

CONCLUSION

Depository institutions are an important part of the U.S. critical infrastructure and as the threats to depository institutions from cyber attacks increase, so does the need for vigilance. Although institutions have been taking steps to protect and defend their systems, the sophistication and technology of the threats and attacks continue to evolve, which challenges institutions (particularly small and medium institutions) and regulators' ability to keep pace with changing risks and threats.

Bank regulators attempt to assess the risk faced by individual institutions and focus their examinations on the areas presenting the highest risks to the safety and soundness of the institution. However, unlike other aspects of institutions' operations, assessing the adequacy of information security practices can produce unique challenges because indicators of problems, such as intrusions, may not be apparent to the institution or the regulator. While regulators devote considerable resources to overseeing information security at larger institutions, limited IT staff resources generally means that examiners with little or no IT expertise are performing IT examinations at smaller institutions. Collecting trend information and analyses could further increase regulators' ability to identify patterns in problems across institutions, better target reviews, and better deploy the IT experts among their staff.

NCUA lacks the authority to examine the third-party technology service providers of credit unions. Having authority to examine third-party service providers would allow NCUA to better monitor the safety and soundness of credit unions. Third-party vendors provide services that are integral to the operations of many credit unions, and deficiencies in their operations could quickly become deficiencies that produce financial and other harm at credit unions. We have long suggested that Congress grant NCUA such authority and maintain that NCUA and smaller credit unions would benefit from this authority.

Matter for Congressional Consideration

To ensure that NCUA has adequate authority to determine the safety and soundness of credit unions, Congress should consider modifying the Federal Credit Union Act to grant NCUA authority to examine technology service providers of credit unions.

Recommendations for Executive Action

To improve their ability to assess the adequacy of the information security practices at medium and small institutions, the heads of FDIC, the Federal Reserve, OCC, and NCUA should routinely categorize IT examination findings and analyze this information to identify trends that can guide areas of review across institutions.

Agency Comments

We provided a draft of this report to DHS, DOJ, FDIC, Federal Reserve, FFIEC, NCUA, OCC, and Treasury. We received written comments from FDIC, Federal Reserve, NCUA, OCC, and Treasury, and technical comments from DHS, FDIC, and Treasury which we incorporated as appropriate.

In its written comments, FDIC agreed that it was important to study IT examination findings to identify trends. In response to our recommendation,

FDIC stated that its staff will explore ways to expand current data tracking and analysis and will work with FFIEC to explore ways to collect and analyze deficiency data across the industry.

The Federal Reserve agreed with our recommendation. In response to our recommendation, the Federal Reserve stated it has been enhancing its processes and capability to categorize and analyze IT examination findings; developing a cyber-event repository to enable more systemic tracking of cyber events; and collaborating on the development of the FFIEC Cybersecurity Assessment Tool, which institutions will use to evaluate their inherent cybersecurity risk and risk-management capabilities.

NCUA stated that it agreed with our report's broad themes, including that more resources should be used to protect deposit-insurance funds and the payment system from cyber threats. Regarding our recommendation and matter for Congressional consideration, NCUA agreed that some of these resources should be devoted to better data collection to enhance cyber-related supervisory policy and practices, and that parity in oversight authority of technology service providers among regulators of depository institutions would help prevent third parties from transmitting material cyber risks to their clients.

OCC stated it appreciated the concerns we raised, and noted recent efforts it and other FFIEC members have undertaken, including creating a FFIEC working group to coordinate sharing of external threat information. In response to our recommendation, OCC said that it has been

integrating the Cybersecurity Assessment Tool into ongoing IT examinations. OCC also recently enhanced its guidance and method for tracking and recording matters requiring attention across its lines of business to help better categorize and monitor such findings.

Finally, Treasury noted that it has been engaged in efforts to improve the timeliness and quality of information shared about cyber threats, and stated that it will continue these efforts.

Lawrance L. Evans, Jr.
Director,
Financial Markets and Community Investment

APPENDIX I: OBJECTIVES, SCOPE, AND METHODOLOGY

In response to high-profile cyber attacks on U.S. institutions, you requested that we study the increased risks depository institutions face due to cyber attacks from criminal organizations and other illicit actors.[1] This report examines (1) cyber attacks on U.S. depository institutions, including the types of threats, impacts, and protective measures taken; (2) the extent to which regulators have provided oversight of depository institutions' actions to mitigate cyber threats; and (3) how depository institutions and their regulators have shared information with other relevant agencies or organizations to identify and address cyber threats.[2]

To obtain information on the types of cyber threats faced by depository institutions, we interviewed information security vendors, bank regulators, federal law enforcement agencies (including the Department of Homeland Security, Department of Justice, and Financial Crimes Enforcement Network), and industry groups.[3] We asked these groups to provide information on the cyber threats depository institutions have faced. We also reviewed and summarized historical information about these threats. To better understand the impact of cyber threats, including costs associated with cyber threats, we reviewed and summarized studies by banking associations and consulting firms about information security threats to depository institutions, how depository institutions defend themselves from attacks, and ongoing issues depository institutions need to address to better defend themselves from attack. We asked the regulators to provide us information on the type and number of cybersecurity incidents depository institutions reported to them from January 2012 to July 2014. To obtain information on the protective measures institutions can and should take, we reviewed regulators' guidance that was issued under the Gramm-Leach-Bliley Act for security programs at depository institutions. We also asked information security vendors about the services they offer to help depository institutions protect themselves and asked the institutions to describe what protective measures they have employed. The information security vendors we interviewed included Battelle, Early Warning Services, the National Cyber-Forensics and Training Alliance, Plante Moran, Prolexic, Trustwave, and Verafin. We reviewed the websites of selected depository institutions to determine the extent to which they provide information to their customers on protecting themselves from information security threats. In general, we clicked on the "Privacy and Security" tab as we determined it was the most likely place for this information. The tab was most often located at the bottom of the homepage. From there, we were able to find various levels of information on information security and steps customers can take to protect themselves.

To determine the extent to which regulators provided oversight of depository institutions' actions to mitigate cyber threats, we reviewed the Information Technology (IT) Examination Handbook of the Federal Financial Institutions Examination Council, with a focus on the Information Security booklet. We reviewed the authority of each bank regulator that requires conducting activities to ensure the safety and soundness of their member institutions. We reviewed a prior GAO report issued in 2011 that compared the guidance in the Handbook with federal guidance (issued by the National Institute of Standards and Technology).[4] We also reviewed bank regulator guidance on information security issued since 2011 to see what additional guidance, if any, the regulators issued to their examiners to address specific IT security threats. We analyzed examination data from 2013 for 15 banks and credit unions. We developed a stratified, non-generalizable sample of 12 institutions (1 large and 11 medium and small) from a list of depository institutions in SNL financial data, stratified by primary regulator and asset size.[5] The remaining three institutions were small and medium-sized banks that the Federal Reserve selected for our review because the examinations involved IT activities.

More specifically, we provided each regulator with a first, second, and third choice of institution for each asset category, by selecting the three institutions closest to the median from the SNL Financial list for each asset size group. If the institution listed as our first choice was not examined for IT in 2013, we asked the regulator to provide materials for the second or third choice, respectively. Only the Office of the Comptroller of the Currency (OCC) was able to provide copies of examination materials for institutions in each asset category from our initial selection. The Federal Deposit Insurance Corporation (FDIC) requested we send an additional sample for the large and medium-sized institutions as none of the institutions we first selected had full IT examinations in 2013. We provided three more options for these two asset categories and FDIC was able to fulfill the document request. The National Credit Union Administration (NCUA) provided copies of exam materials from our original request list, but only the large credit union had any IT functions. Therefore, we requested copies of exam materials for the two additional large credit unions that were included in our original request and NCUA provide these to us.

The Board of Governors of the Federal Reserve System (Federal Reserve) initially provided us copies of examination reports for institutions not included on our request list because, as with FDIC, the institutions on our list did not have IT examinations for 2013. To preserve the independence of our review, we requested, and the Federal Reserve provided, a list of all the institutions they examined for IT in 2013. From this list, we selected three institutions for which we received copies of the examination materials. As a result, in this review, we analyzed six institutions that were examined for IT by the Federal Reserve. In some instances, the examinations led by the Federal Reserve were jointly conducted with a state regulator, in which case the Federal Reserve received permission to share the report with us.

We also reviewed examinations conducted in 2013 for a random selection of seven IT service providers that provide core processing and other services to depository institutions to determine the extent to which these companies were supervised for information security risks. We obtained these examinations from the lead regulator, which in the case of the examinations we selected was either FDIC or the Federal Reserve. We reviewed the examinations to determine what steps examiners took during the examination and the types of deficiencies they identified.

We also reviewed aggregated data provided by the regulators on the number of bank IT examinations and the number of deficiencies regulators identified in these examinations. We analyzed the extent to which regulators considered the aggregated data in light of federal internal control standards.[6] These standards indicate that entities should have relevant, reliable, and timely information on key agency activities. The standards also state that key information on an entity's operations should be recorded and communicated to management and others within the entity and within a time frame that enables management to carry out its internal control and other responsibilities. These standards apply to federal agencies, including the banking regulators. To determine the reliability of these data, we reviewed information about the systems used to collect the data and agency statements on how the data were prepared. We determined that data were sufficiently reliable for our purposes.

To assess how depository institutions receive and share information about cyber threats, and the type of information they need to adequately prepare for these threats, we held three conference calls with a group of approximately 50 large, medium, and small financial institutions arranged through two industry associations: the Financial Services Roundtable's BITS and the Independent Community Bankers of America.[7] BITS shares its membership with the Financial Services Roundtable, and its members are among the 150 largest U.S. financial services companies based on market capitalization. The Independent Community Bankers of America represents more than 6,000 community banks. We intended to meet with officials from the institutions for which we received examination materials from the bank regulators to learn how they defend themselves against cyber attacks. However, only one of the institutions we contacted agreed to our interview request. We interviewed a second institution that we selected from our broader SNL Financial list. We interviewed officials and reviewed the information security websites of federal agencies to determine the extent to which they provide information to depository institutions or the public about information security threats or protection steps. We reviewed information from the Financial Services Information Sharing and Analysis Center—a nonprofit entity serving as a resource for cyber and physical threat intelligence and analysis for the global financial industry—on the types of threat information it provides to depository institutions. We also reviewed the Suspicious Activity Report form—on which financial sector institutions report potential criminal activity to the Department of the Treasury—to determine the extent to which the form captures cyber-related information. Lastly, we reviewed and summarized information in prior GAO reports about challenges and recommendations for improved information sharing for information security.[3]

We conducted this performance audit from February 2014 to July 2015 in accordance with generally accepted government auditing standards. Those standards require that we plan and perform the audit to obtain sufficient, appropriate evidence to provide a reasonable basis for our findings and conclusions based on our audit objectives. We believe that the evidence obtained provides a reasonable basis for our findings and conclusions based on our audit objectives.

APPENDIX II: CYBERSECURITY GUIDANCE APPLICABLE TO THE BANKING AND FINANCE SECTOR

This appendix contains a table listing cybersecurity guidance identified as applicable to entities within the banking and finance sector. This list was originally published in GAO, Critical Infrastructure Protection: Cybersecurity Guidance Is Available, but More Can Be Done to Promote Its Use, GAO-12-92 (Washington, D.C.: Dec. 9, 2011), and has been updated for purposes of this report. This list should not be considered to include all cybersecurity guidance that may be available or used within the banking and finance sector.

Table 4. Cybersecurity Guidance Applicable to the Banking and Finance Sector

1.	Federal Financial Institutions Examination Council (FFIEC), IT Examination Handbook, December 2004.
2.	FFIEC, Supplement to Authentication in an Internet Banking Environment, June 2011.
3.	FFIEC, IT Examination Handbook, "Outsourcing Technology Services Booklet," Appendix D, Managing Security Service Providers, April 3, 2012
4.	FFIEC, IT Examination Handbook, Outsourcing Technology Services Booklet, April 12, 2012.
5.	FFIEC, IT Examination Handbook, Audit Booklet, May 7, 2012.
6.	FFIEC, IT Examination Handbook, Business Continuity Planning Booklet, May 7, 2012.
7.	FFIEC, IT Examination Handbook, E-Banking Booklet, May 7, 2012.
8.	FFIEC, IT Examination Handbook, Information Security Booklet, May 7, 2012.
9.	FFIEC, IT Examination Handbook, Operations Booklet, May 7, 2012.
10.	FFIEC, IT Examination Handbook, Retail Payment Systems Booklet, May 7, 2012.
11.	FFIEC, IT Examination Handbook, Supervision of Technology Service Providers Booklet, May 7, 2012.
12.	FFIEC, Outsourcing Cloud Computing, July 10, 2012.
13.	FFIEC, Implementation of Interagency Programs for the Supervision of Technology Service Providers, October 31, 2012.
14.	FFIEC, Joint Statement: Cyber-attacks on Financial Institutions' ATM and Card Authorization Systems, April 2, 2014.
15.	FFIEC, Joint Statement: Distributed Denial-of-Service Cyber-attacks, Risk Mitigation, and Additional Resources, April 2, 2014.
16.	Board of Governors of the Federal Reserve System (Federal Reserve), Guidance on Managing Outsourcing Risk, December 5, 2013.
17.	Federal Reserve, Supervision and Regulation (SR) Letter 12-14, Revised Guidance on Supervision of Technology ServiceProviders, October 31, 2012.
18.	Federal Reserve, SR Letter 11-9, Interagency Supplement to Authentication in an Internet Banking Environment, June 29, 2011.
19.	Federal Reserve, SR Letter 10-3, FFIEC Retail Payment Systems Booklet, February 26, 2010.
20.	Federal Reserve, SR Letter 09-2, FFIEC Guidance Addressing Risk Management of Remote Deposit Capture Activities, January 14, 2009.
21.	Federal Reserve, SR Letter 06-12, FFIEC Information Security Booklet, July 28, 2006.

22.	Federal Reserve, SR Letter 05-23/CA 05-10, Interagency Guidance on Response Programs for Unauthorized Access to Customer Information and Customer Notice, December 1, 2005.
23.	Federal Reserve, SR Letter 05-19, Interagency Guidance on Authentication in an Internet Banking Environment, October 13, 2005.
24.	Federal Reserve, SR Letter 04-17, FFIEC Guidance on the use of Free and Open Source Software, December 6, 2004.
25.	Federal Reserve, SR Letter 04-14, FFIEC Brochure with Information on Internet "Phishing," October 19, 2004.
26.	Federal Reserve, SR Letter 02-18, Section 312 of the USA Patriot Act—Due Diligence for Correspondent and Private Banking Accounts, July 23, 2002.
27.	Federal Reserve, SR Letter 02-6, Information Sharing Pursuant to Section 314(b) of the USA Patriot Act, March 14, 2002.
28.	Federal Reserve, SR Letter 01-15, Standards for Safeguarding Customer Information, May 31, 2001.
29.	Federal Reserve, SR Letter 01-11, Identity Theft and Pretext Calling, April 26, 2001.
30.	Federal Reserve, SR Letter 00-17, Guidance on the Risk Management of Outsourced Technology Services, November 30, 2000.
31.	Federal Reserve, SR Letter 00-04, Outsourcing of Information and Transaction Processing, February 29, 2000.
32.	Federal Reserve, SR Letter 99-08, Uniform Rating System for Information Technology, March 31, 1999.
33.	Federal Reserve, SR Letter 97-32, Sound Practices Guidance for Information Security for Networks, December 4, 1997.
34.	Federal Deposit Insurance Corporation (FDIC), Financial Institution Letter FIL-16-2014, Technology Alert: OpenSSL "Heartbleed" Vulnerability, April 11, 2014.
35.	FDIC, FIL-13-2014, Technology Outsourcing: Informational Tools for Community Bankers, April 7, 2014.
36.	FDIC, FIL-11-2014, Distributed Denial of Service (DDoS) Attacks, April 2, 2014.
37.	FDIC, FIL-10-2014, ATM and Card Authorization Systems, April 2, 2014.
38.	FDIC, FIL-3-2012, Payment Processor Relationships, Revised Guidance, January 31, 2012.
39.	FDIC, FIL-50-2011, FFIEC Supplement to Authentication in an Internet Banking Environment, June 29, 2011.
40.	FDIC, FIL-56-2010, Guidance on Mitigating Risk Posed by Information Stored on Photocopiers, Fax Machines, and Printers,September 15, 2010.
41.	FDIC, FIL-6-2010, Retail Payment Systems Booklet, Update to FFIEC IT Examination Handbook Series, February 25, 2010.
42.	FDIC, FIL-30-2009, Identify Theft Red Flags, Address Discrepancies, and Change of Address Regulations, Frequently Asked Questions, June 11, 2009.

Table 4. (Continued)

43.	FDIC, FIL-4-2009, Risk Management of Remote Deposit Capture, January 14, 2009.
44.	FDIC, FIL-127-2008, Guidance on Payment Processor Relationships, November 7, 2008.
45.	FDIC, FIL-44-2008, Third-Party Risk, Guidance for Managing Third-Party Risk, June 6, 2008.
46.	FDIC, FIL-100-2007, Identity Theft Red Flags, Interagency Final Regulation and Guidelines, November 15, 2007.
47.	FDIC, FIL-32-2007, Identity Theft, FDIC's Supervisory Policy on Identity Theft, April 11, 2007.
48.	FDIC, FIL-77-2006, Authentication in an Internet Banking Environment, Frequently Asked Questions, August 21, 2006.
49.	FDIC, FIL-52-2006, Foreign-Based Third-Party Service Providers, Guidance on Managing Risks in These Outsourcing Relationships, June 21, 2006.
50.	FDIC, FIL-103-2005, FFIEC Guidance: Authentication in an Internet Banking Environment, October 12, 2005.
51.	FDIC, FIL-66-2005, Spyware - Guidance on Mitigating Risks from Spyware, July 22, 2005.
52.	FDIC, FIL-64-2005, Guidance on How Financial Institutions Can Protect against Pharming Attacks, July 18, 2005.
53.	FDIC, FIL-59-2005, Identity Theft Study Supplement on "Account-Hijacking Identity Theft," July 5, 2005.
54.	FDIC, FIL-46-2005, Pre-Employment Background Screening: Guidance on Developing an Effective Pre-Employment Background Screening Process.
55.	FDIC, FIL-27-2005, Final Guidance on Response Programs for Unauthorized Access to Customer Information and Customer Notice, April 1, 2005.
56.	FDIC, FIL-7-2005, Fair and Accurate Credit Transactions Act of 2003 Guidelines Requiring the Proper Disposal of Customer Information, February 2, 2005.
57.	FDIC, FIL-132-2004, Identity Theft Study on "Account-Hijacking" Identity Theft and Suggestions for Reducing Online Fraud, December 14, 2004.
58.	FDIC, FIL-121-2004, Computer Software Due Diligence - Guidance on Developing an Effective Software Evaluation Program to Assure Quality and Regulatory Compliance, November 16, 2004.
59.	FDIC, FIL-114-2004, Risk Management of Free and Open Source Software FFIEC Guidance.
60.	FDIC, FIL-103-2004, Interagency Informational Brochure on Internet "Phishing" Scams, September 13, 2004.
61.	FDIC, FIL-84-2004, Guidance on Instant Messaging, July 21, 2004.
62.	FDIC, FIL-62-2004, Guidance on Developing an Effective Computer Virus Protection Program, June 7, 2004.

63.	FDIC, FIL-27-2004, Guidance on Safeguarding Customers against E-Mail and Internet Related Fraudulent Schemes, March12, 2004
64.	FDIC, FIL-63-2003, Guidance on Identity Theft Response Programs, August 13, 2003.
65.	FDIC, FIL-43-2003, Guidance on Developing an Effective Software Patch Management Program, May 29, 2003.
66.	FDIC, FIL-8-2002, Wireless Networks and Customer Access, February 1, 2002.
67.	FDIC, FIL-69-2001, Authentication in an Electronic Banking Environment, August 24, 2001.
68.	FDIC, FIL-68-2001, 501(b) Examination Guidance, August 24, 2001.
69.	FDIC, FIL-39-2001, Guidance on Identity Theft and Pretext Calling, May 9, 2001.
70.	FDIC, FIL-22-2001, Security Standards for Customer Information, March 14, 2001.
71.	FDIC, FIL-77-2000, Bank Technology Bulletin: Protecting Internet Domain Names, November 9, 2000.
72.	FDIC, FIL-67-2000, Security Monitoring of Computer Networks, October 3, 2000.
73.	FDIC, FIL-68-99, Risk Assessment Tools and Practices for Information System Security, July 7, 1999.
74.	FDIC, FIL-98-98, Pretext Phone Calling, September 2, 1998.
75.	FDIC, FIL-131-97, Security Risks Associated with the Internet, December 18, 1997.
76.	FDIC, FIL-124-97, Suspicious Activity Reporting, December 5, 1997.
77.	FDIC, FIL-82-96, Risks Involving Client/Server Computer Systems, October 8, 1996.
78.	National Credit Union Administration (NCUA), Letter to Credit Unions 15-CU-01, Supervisory Priorities for 2015, January 2015.
79.	NCUA, Letter to Credit Unions 14-CU-02, Supervisory Focus for 2014, January 2014.
80.	NCUA, Risk Alert 13-CU-01, Mitigating Distributed Denial-of-Service Attacks, February 2013.
81.	NCUA, Letter to Credit Unions 13-CU-01, Supervisory Focus for 2013, January 2013.
82.	NCUA, Letter to Credit Unions 11-CU-09, Online Member Authentication Guidance, June 2011.
83.	NCUA, Letter to Credit Unions 09-CU-01, Risk Management of Remote Deposit Capture, January 2009.
84.	NCUA, Letter to Credit Unions 06-CU-13, Frequently Asked Questions on FFIEC Guidance on Authentication in an Internet Banking Environment, August 2006.
85.	NCUA, Letter to Credit Unions 05-CU-20, Phishing Guidance for Credit Unions and Their Members, December 2005.

Table 4. (Continued)

86.	NCUA, Letter to Credit Unions 05-CU-18, Guidance on Authentication in Internet Banking Environment, November 2005.
87.	NCUA, Letter to Credit Unions 04-CU-12, Phishing Guidance for Credit Union Members, September 2004.
88.	NCUA, Letter to Credit Unions 04-CU-06, E-Mail and Internet Related Fraudulent Schemes Guidance, April 2004.
89.	NCUA, Letter to Credit Unions 04-CU-05, Fraudulent E-Mail Schemes, April 2004.
90.	NCUA, Letter to Credit Unions 03-CU-14, Computer Software Patch Management, September 2003.
91.	NCUA, Letter to Credit Unions 03-CU-12, Fraudulent Newspaper Advertisements, and Websites by Entities Claiming to beCredit Unions, August 2003.
92.	NCUA, Letter to Credit Unions 03-CU-08, Weblinking: Identifying Risks and Risk Management Techniques, April 2003.
93.	NCUA, Letter to Credit Unions 03-CU-03, Wireless Technology, February 2003.
94.	NCUA, Letter to Federal Credit Unions 02-FCU-11, Tips to Safely Conduct Financial Transactions over the Internet—An NCUA Brochure for Credit Union Members, July 2002.
95.	NCUA, Letter to Credit Unions 02-CU-13, Vendor Information Systems and Technology Reviews—Summary Results, July 2002.
96.	NCUA, Letter to Credit Unions 02-CU-08, Account Aggregation Services, April 2002.
97.	NCUA, Letter to Federal Credit Unions 02-FCU-04, Weblinking Relationships, March 2002.
98.	NCUA, Letter to Credit Unions 01-CU-21, Disaster Recovery and Business Resumption Contingency Plans, December 2001.
99.	NCUA, Letter to Credit Unions 01-CU-20, Due Diligence over Third-Party Service Providers, November 2001.
100.	NCUA, Letter to Credit Unions 01-CU-12, E-Commerce Insurance Considerations, October 2001.
101.	NCUA, Letter to Credit Unions 01-CU-09, Identity Theft and Pretext Calling, September 2001.
102.	NCUA, Letter to Credit Unions 01-CU-11, Electronic Data Security Overview, August 2001.
103.	NCUA, Letter to Credit Unions 01-CU-10, Authentication in an Electronic Banking Environment, August 2001.
104.	NCUA, Letter to Credit Unions 01-CU-04, Integrating Financial Services and Emerging Technology, March 2001.
105.	NCUA, Regulatory Alert 01-RA-03, Electronic Signatures in Global and National Commerce Act (E-Sign Act), March 2001.

106.	NCUA, Letter to Credit Unions 01-CU-02, Privacy of Consumer Financial Information, February 2001.
107.	NCUA, Letter to Credit Unions 00-CU-11, Risk Management of Outsourced Technology Services (with Enclosure), December 2000.
108.	NCUA, Letter to Credit Unions 00-CU-07, NCUA's Information Systems and Technology Examination Program, October 2000.
109.	NCUA, Letter to Credit Unions 00-CU-04, Suspicious Activity Reporting (see section on "Computer Intrusion"), July 2000.
110.	NCUA, Letter to Credit Unions 00-CU-02, Identity Theft Prevention, May 2000.
111.	NCUA, Regulatory Alert 99-RA-3, Pretext Phone Calling by Account Information Brokers, February 1999.
112.	NCUA, Regulatory Alert 98-RA-4, Interagency Guidance on Electronic Financial Services and Consumer Compliance, July1998.
113.	NCUA, Letter to Credit Unions 97-CU-5, Interagency Statement on Retail On-Line PC Banking, April 1997.
114.	NCUA, Letter to Credit Unions 97-CU-1, Automated Response System Controls, January 1997.
115.	NCUA, Letter to Credit Unions 109, Information Processing Issues, September 1989.
116.	Office of the Comptroller of the Currency (OCC), Bulletin 2014-14, Distributed Denial-of-Service Cyber Attacks, Risk Mitigation, and Additional Resources: Joint Statement, April 3, 2014.
117.	OCC, Bulletin 2013-29, Third-Party Relationships: Risk Management Guidance, October 30, 2013.
118.	OCC, Alert 2012-16, Information Security: Distributed Denial- o- Service Attacks and Customer Account Fraud, December 21, 2012.
119.	OCC, Bulletin 2012-34, Supervision of Technology Service Providers: FFIEC IT Examination Handbook Booklet Revision and Administrative Guidelines for Interagency Supervisory Programs, October 31, 2012.
120.	OCC, Bulletin 2011-27, Prepaid Access Programs: Risk Management Guidance and Sound Practices, June 28, 2011.
121.	OCC, Bulletin 2011-26, Authentication in an Internet Banking Environment: Supplement, June 28, 2011.
122.	OCC, Consumer Advisory CA 2011-2, Avoiding "Card Skimming" at ATMs and Other Money Machines, June 1, 2011.
123.	OCC, Alert 2011-4, Incident Prevention and Detection: Protecting Information Security of National Banks, April 18, 2011.
124.	OCC, Bulletin 2010-9, FFIEC IT Examination Handbook: Retail Payment Systems Booklet, February 25, 2010.
125.	OCC Bulletin 2009-4, Remote Deposit Capture: Interagency Guidance, January 14, 2009.
126.	OCC, Bulletin 2008-16, Information Security: Application Security, May 8, 2008.

Table 4. (Continued)

127.	OCC, Bulletin 2007-45, Identity Theft Red Flags and Address Discrepancies, November 14, 2007.
28.	OCC, Alert 2006-50, Customer Authentication and Internet Banking Alert, September 8, 2006
129.	OCC, Bulletin 2006-39, Automated Clearing House Activities: Risk Management Guidance, September 1, 2006.
130.	OCC, Bulletin 2006-31, FFIEC Information Security Booklet, July 27, 2006.
131.	OCC, Bulletin 2005-44, Small Entity Compliance Guide: Information Security, December 14, 2005.
132.	OCC, Bulletin 2005-35, Authentication in an Internet Banking Environment, October 2005.
133.	OCC, Bulletin 2005-24, Threats from Fraudulent Bank Web Sites: Risk Mitigation and Response Guidance for Web Site Spoofing Incidents, July 2005.
134.	OCC, Bulletin 2005-13, Response Programs for Unauthorized Access to Customer Information and Customer Notice: FinalGuidance, April 2005.
135.	OCC, Bulletin 2005-1, Proper Disposal of Customer Information, January 2005.
136.	OCC, Bulletin 2003-27, Suspicious Activity Report-Revised Form, June 2003.
137.	OCC, Advisory 2003-10, Risk Management of Wireless Networks, December 2003.
138.	OCC, Alert 2003-11, Customer Identity Theft: E-Mail-Related Fraud Threats, September 2003.
139.	OCC, Bulletin 2001-47, Third-Party Relationships Risk Management Principles, November 2001.
140.	OCC, Bulletin 2001-35, Examination Procedures for Guidelines to Safeguard Customer Information, July 2001.
141.	OCC, Alert 2001-04, Network Security Vulnerabilities, April 2001.
142.	OCC, Bulletin 2001-12, Bank-Provided Account Aggregation Services: Guidance to Banks, February 2001.
143.	OCC, Bulletin 2001-8, Guidelines Establishing Standards for Safeguarding Customer Information, February 2001.
144.	OCC, Alert 2000-9, Protecting Internet Addresses of National Banks, July 2000.
145.	OCC, Bulletin 2000-19, Suspicious Activity Report: New SAR Form, June 2000.
146.	OCC, Bulletin 2000-14, Infrastructure Threats—Intrusion Risks: Message to Bankers and Examiners, May 2000.
147.	OCC, Alert 2000-1, Internet Security: Distributed Denial of Service Attacks, February 2000.
148.	OCC, Bulletin 99-20, Certificate Authority Guidance: Guidance for Bankers

	and Examiners, May 1999.
149.	OCC, Bulletin 98-3, Technology Risk Management: Guidance for Bankers and Examiners, February 1998.
150.	Payment Card Industry Data Security Standard (PCI-DSS), Version 3.1, April 2015.
151.	National Institute of Standards and Technology (NIST), SP 800-53, Revision 4, Security and Privacy Controls for Federal Information Systems and Organizations, April 30, 2013.
152.	NIST, Framework for Improving Critical Infrastructure Cybersecurity, Version 1.0, February 12, 2014.

Source: GAO analysis, Federal Reserve, FDIC, NCUA, and OCC. | GAO-15-509

Note: This list should not be considered to include all cybersecurity guidance that may be available or used within the banking and finance sector.

End Notes

[1] A data breach or disclosure may be defined as any event resulting in confirmed compromise (unauthorized viewing or accessing) of any non-public information.

[2] FSOC was established to identify risks to the financial stability of the United States, promote market discipline, and respond to emerging threats to the stability of the financial system. Pub. L. No. 111-203, § 112(a)(1), 124 Stat. 1376, 1394 (2010) (codified at 12 U.S.C. § 5322(a)(1)). FSOC, which is chaired by the Secretary of the Department of the Treasury, consists of 15 members and includes the heads of the Board of Governors of the Federal Reserve System, Federal Deposit Insurance Corporation, Office of the Comptroller of the Currency, National Credit Union Administration, and Securities and Exchange Commission. § 111(b), 124 Stat. at 1392-93 (codified at 12 U.S.C. § 5321(b)).

[3] GAO, *High-Risk Series: An Update*, GAO-15-290 (Washington, D.C.; Feb. 14, 2015).

[4] We anticipate that this report will be the first in a series examining cybersecurity in the financial services sector. As a result, this report addresses cybersecurity issues facing depository institutions and only briefly discusses cyber threats to payment systems or card networks. We plan to address cyber threats to the payment card markets, securities market participants, and insurance firms in subsequent reports.

[5] In this report, we refer to the regulators of depository institutions (banks, thrifts, and credit unions) and their holding companies as bank regulators. See table 1. The Bureau of Consumer Financial Protection is responsible for examining depository institutions with total assets greater than $10 billion for compliance with consumer protection laws, but we did not review the Bureau's activities for this report.

[6] We reviewed examination data from 12 selected depository institutions based on data from SNL Financial, a financial data and analysis company, listed by primary regulator and asset size. In some instances, the institutions we selected had not been examined for IT during 2013. In those instances, we selected another institution from a list provided by the regulator of institutions examined for IT during 2013. One smaller institution we interviewed was selected from our broader SNL Financial list. We reviewed the 2013 examinations for these institutions because 2014 data were not available at the time of our request. In addition to the 12 we selected, 1 regulator also provided three additional examinations that it had

selected because IT issues had been a part of the focus of the examinations. See appendix 1 for more information.

[7] GAO, *Standards for Internal Control in the Federal Government*, GAO/AIMD-00.21.3.1 (Washington, D.C.: November 1999).

[8] Critical infrastructures are systems and assets, whether physical or virtual, so vital to our nation that their incapacity or destruction would have a debilitating impact on national security, economic well-being, public health or safety, or any combination of these.

[9] Homeland Security Act of 2002, Pub. L. No. 107-296, 116 Stat. 2135 (codified at 6 U.S.C. §§ 101-629); The White House, *Critical Infrastructure Security and Resilience*, Presidential Policy Directive 21 (Washington, D.C.: Feb. 12, 2013); and Department of Homeland Security, *National Infrastructure Protection Plan: Partnering for Critical Infrastructure Security and Resilience* (Washington, D.C.: 2013).

[10] Pub. L. No. 107-296, § 102(f)(7) and § 201(d)(5), (9), 116 Stat. 2135, 2144, and 2146 (codified at 6 U.S.C. § 112(f)(7) and § 121(d)(5), (9)). Presidential Policy Directive 21 established 16 critical infrastructure sectors: food and agriculture; financial services; chemical; commercial facilities; communications; critical manufacturing; dams; defense industrial base; emergency services; energy; government facilities; information technology; nuclear reactors, materials, and waste; health care and public health; transportation systems; and water and wastewater systems.

[11] The National Cybersecurity Communications and Integration Center was codified as a center within DHS by the National Cybersecurity Protection Act of 2014, Pub. L. No. 113- 282, § 3(a), 128 Stat. 3066, 3066-3067 (codified at 6 U.S.C. § 148(b)).

[12] 31 C.F.R. § 1020.320(a).

[13] FS-ISAC, established by the financial services sector, collaborates with Treasury and others to enhance the ability of the financial services sector around the globe to prepare for and respond to cyber and physical threats, vulnerabilities and incidents, and to serve as the primary communications channel for the sector. We discuss its activities later in this report.

[14] JPMorgan Chase & Co., Current Report (Form 8-K) (Oct. 2, 2014).

[15] See *Patco Const. Co. v. People's United Bank*, 684 F.3d 197 (1st Cir. 2012).

[16] See 12 C.F.R. pts. 30 and 364, App. B and pt. 225, App. F.

[17] SNL Financial provides news, data, and analysis on business and financial sectors. For example, it aggregates and provides, by subscription, data from quarterly regulatory reports.

[18] In the study, per capita cost was defined as the total cost of the data breach divided by the size of the data breach (the number of lost or stolen records). To calculate the average cost of the data breach, the study included direct and indirect expenses incurred by the organization, such as engaging forensic experts, providing free credit monitoring, and in-house investigations. Ponemon Institute, *2014 Cost of Data Breach Study: Global Analysis* (May 2014).

[19] Center for Strategic and International Studies, *The Economic Impact of Cybercrime and Cyber Espionage* (July 2013).

[20] SANS Institute, *Risk, Loss and Security Spending in the Financial Sector: A SANS Survey* (March 2014).

[21] Center for Strategic and International Studies, *The Economic Impact of Cybercrime and Cyber Espionage* (July 2013).

[22] The impact of recent security incidents and data breaches on depository institutions' stock prices is unclear.

[23] The Insurance Information Institute has been a source of information, analysis, and referral concerning insurance for more than 50 years.

[24] FFIEC is a formal interagency body empowered to prescribe uniform principles, standards, and report forms for the federal examination of financial institutions by the agencies that compose the FFIEC and to make recommendations to promote uniformity in the supervision of financial institutions. The constituent agencies are the Federal Reserve, FDIC, NCUA, OCC, Bureau of Consumer Financial Protection, and the State Liaison Committee, which consists of five representatives from state regulatory agencies that supervise financial institutions.

[25] See GAO, *Critical Infrastructure Protection: Cybersecurity Guidance Is Available, but More Can Be Done to Promote Its Use*, GAO-12-92 (Washington, D.C.: Dec. 9, 2011) for our comparison of the FFIEC IT Examination Handbook with National Institute of Standards and Technology, *Recommended Security Controls for Federal Information Systems and Organizations,* SP 800.53, rev. 3 (Gaithersburg, Md.: May 2010). In the 2011 report (see app. II), we listed cybersecurity guidance applicable to the banking and finance sector as of the report date. In this report, we present an updated the list of cybersecurity guidance applicable to depository institutions.

[26] The National Institute of Standards and Technology develops and promotes measurement, standards, and technology to enhance productivity, facilitate trade, and improve quality of life. Executive Order 13636 called for the development of a voluntary risk-based cybersecurity framework—a set of industry standards and best practices to help organizations manage cybersecurity risks. Executive Order 13636—Improving Critical Infrastructure Cybersecurity, 78 Fed. Reg. 11739 (Feb. 19, 2013) We did not assess the extent to which the bank regulators' guidance conforms to the updated federal guidance.

[27] Pub. L. No. 106-102, § 501(b), 113 Stat. 1338, 1436-37 (1999) (codified at 15 U.S.C. § 6801(b)).

[28] Interagency Guidelines Establishing Standards for Safeguarding Customer Information and Rescission of Year 2000 Standards for Safety and Soundness, 66 Fed. Reg. 8616 (Feb. 1, 2001). Under the guidelines, the elements of an institution's information security program mandated by the Gramm-Leach-Bliley Act encompass an annual risk assessment that includes identifying possible internal and external threats; risk management and control, which includes designing the information security program to control the identified risks; and oversight of technology service provider agreements. Institutions were also to adjust their information security programs as appropriate; report to the board of directors at least annually on the status of the program; and ensure board involvement, including having the board review the information security program and oversee the development and implementation of the program. 12 C.F.R. pt. 30, App. B.

[29] See 12 C.F.R. pt. 364, App. B, supp. A. (FDIC); 12 C.F.R. pt. 208, App. D-2. (Federal Reserve); 12 C.F.R. pt. 30, App. B, supp. A (OCC); and 12 C.F.R. pt. 748, App. B (NCUA).

[30] Joint Statement: Distributed Denial-of-Service (DDoS) Cyber-Attacks, Risk Mitigation, and Additional Resources (Apr. 2, 2014).

[31] OpenSSL "Heartbleed" Vulnerability Alert (Apr. 10, 2014). The vulnerability known as OpenSSL "Heartbleed" was a flaw in the software used to encrypt some information sent over the Internet. The "Heartbleed" bug would allow anyone on the Internet to read the memory of the systems using the flawed version of the OpenSSL software.

[32] The regulators examine the safety and soundness of depository institutions on a regular cycle, with some very large institutions being continuously examined and most other institutions being examined every 12 to 18 months.

[33] 12 U.S.C. § 1820(b) (FDIC); 12 U.S.C. § 1(a) (OCC); 12 U.S.C. § 248(a) and 12 U.S.C. § 1844(c) (Federal Reserve); and 12 U.S.C. § 1786(b) (NCUA).

[34] This group consists of representatives from FFIEC member agencies and has been working to enhance communication among these agencies on critical infrastructure and cybersecurity issues.

[35] We categorized depository institutions as large if they had assets of $50 billion or more; medium, from $1 billion to less than $50 billion; and small, less than $1 billion. We reviewed examination materials for 15 examinations but 1 examination conducted at a very large institution only focused on the steps the institution took in the aftermath of the DDOS attacks experienced by several large institutions. For the other 14 examinations, the institutions had total assets ranging from $87 million to $24.9 billion. The examination materials provided included reports of examination, scoping documents and other examiner work papers, and in some instances, documents provided by the institution to the examiner, including information security programs, risk assessments, and external audit reports.

[36] Specifically, the external audit looked at internal network security, including server-specific testing and vulnerability scanning; information security controls, including incident response plans and testing; network administrative review; core application controls; distributed application controls; e-banking controls; business continuity planning; physical security environment; desktop management and support; program change and documentation controls; technology service provider management; and compliance with Gramm-Leach-Bliley provisions.

[37] FDIC told us that it conducted 64 examinations of institutions with highly complex IT infrastructure that required one or more premium IT examiners in 2014.

[38] IT examination analysts have specialized IT skills and participate on less-complex IT examinations. Subject-matter experts are commissioned examiners who have completed additional IT training and conduct more complex IT examinations. In addition, each FDIC region has two to three IT examination specialists to oversee IT examinations.

[39] Examiners are assigned full-time to 1 of the 19 institutions in the large bank program. The number of IT specialists assigned to a particular institution will vary depending on the size and complexity of the institution.

[40] Generalist examiners will typically conduct IT examinations of lower-risk community institutions at which core processing is outsourced to a third-party technology service provider.

[41] FFIEC also announced an enhanced incident analysis process, an updated crisis management process, an expanded focus on technology service providers, and enhanced collaboration with law enforcement and intelligence agencies.

[42] GAO, *Standards for Internal Control in the Federal Government*, GAO/AIMD-00.21.3.1 (Washington, D.C.; November, 1999).

[43] FDIC officials reported that when deficiencies are material enough to warrant a citation in the Matters Requiring Board Attention section of the examination report, they are tracked in a database to ensure timely follow up of corrective actions.

[44] See 12 C.F.R. p. 364, App. B, supp. A, II.A.1.b. (FDIC); 12 C.F.R. pt. 208, App. D2.II.A.1.b. (Federal Reserve); 12 C.F.R. pt. 30, App. B, supp. A, II.A.1.b. (OCC); and 12 C.F.R. pt. 748, App. B, II.A.1.b. (NCUA). This interagency guidance was issued in response to the Gramm-Leach-Bliley Act requirement that the federal banking regulators establish appropriate standards for the financial institutions subject to their jurisdictions to insure the security and confidentiality of customer records and information and to protect against unauthorized access to or use of those records or information that could result in substantial harm or inconvenience to customers. Pub. L. No. 106-103, § 501(b), 113 Stat. 1338, 1437 (1999) (codified at 15 U.S.C. § 6801(b)).

[45] See GAO, *Risk-Focused Bank Examinations: Regulators of Large Banking Organizations Face Challenges*, GAO-GGD-00-48 (Washington, D.C.: Jan. 24, 2000).

[46] See GAO, *Bank Secrecy Act: Suspicious Activity Report Use is Increasing, but FinCEN Needs to Further Develop and Document Its Form Revision Process*, GAO-09-226 (Washington, D.C.: Feb. 27, 2009).

[47] See GAO, *Credit Unions: Financial Condition Has Improved, but Opportunities Exist to Enhance Oversight and Share Insurance Management*, GAO-04-91 (Washington, D.C.: Oct. 27, 2003). This report examined the financial condition of the credit union industry and the Share Insurance Fund, the impact of the Credit Union Membership Access Act on the industry; and how NCUA changed its safety and soundness processes. We discussed NCUA's lack of authority to examine third-party vendors in relation to a broader finding that NCUA faced challenges in implementing its risk-focused examination and supervision program.

[48] Pub. L. No. 87-856, § 5, 76 Stat. 1132, 1133 (1962) (codified as amended at 12 U.S.C. 1867(c).

[49] Pub. L. No. 111-203, §§ 1024(e), 1025(d), and 1026(e), 124 Stat. 1376, 1990-1995 (2010) (codified at 12 U.S.C. §§ 5515(e), 5515(d), and 5516(e)).

[50] Pub. L. No. 73-467, 48 Stat. 1215 (1934) (codified as amended at 12 U.S.C. §§ 1751- 1795k). See also Examination Parity and Year 2000 Readiness for Financial Institutions Act, Pub. L. No. 105-164, § 3(b), 112 Stat. 32, 35 (1998).

[51] These are known as Matters Requiring Attention, which are findings that are deemed sufficiently important that the institution must take corrective actions within a specified period of time.

[52] GAO, *Electronic Banking: Enhancing Oversight of Internet Banking Activities*, GAO/GGD-99-91 (Washington, D.C.: July 6, 1999).

[53] See GAO-04-91.

[54] We closed this matter as not implemented in July 2008.

[55] ISACs have been formed for the following sectors: (1) aviation; (2) defense industrial base; (3) emergency services; (4) electricity; (5) financial services; (6) information technology; (7) maritime security; (8) communications; (9) multistate; (10) national health; (11) oil and gas; (12) public transit; (13) real estate; (14) research and education; (15) supply chain; (16) surface transportation; and (17) water.

[56] These traffic light protocol codes were effective as of April 2014.

[57] The Depository Trust and Clearing Corporation is a centralized clearinghouse and securities depository for securities exchanges and trading platforms in the United States.

[58] Many news-related websites, blogs, and other online publishers use rich site summary, a format for delivering regularly changing Internet content. Bulletin boards are online discussion sites on a broad range of subject areas, which themselves contain more specific subject areas (forums) with conversations on a particular topic (threads).

[59] The integration center was codified as a center within DHS by the National Cybersecurity Protection Act of 2014, Pub. L. No. 113-282, § 3(a), 128 Stat. 3066, 3067 (codified at 6 U.S.C. § 148(b)).

[60] See 12 C.F.R. pt. 364, App. B, supp. A. (FDIC); 12 C.F.R. pt. 208, App. D-2. (Federal Reserve); 12 C.F.R. pt. 30, App. B, supp. A (OCC); and 12 C.F.R. pt. 748, App. B (NCUA).

[61] According to this organization, the states with no security breach law were Alabama, New Mexico, and South Dakota.

[62] See 6 U.S.C. § 133(a)(1)(D).

[63] Threat vectors might be fake websites or e-mails, mobile devices, social networking websites, or malware.

[64] See Homeland Security Information Network, *HSIN Financial Service (FS) Portal Quick Guide*, accessed on April 20, 2015, available at http://go.usa.gov/3YH45.

End Notes for Appendix I

[1] Cyber attacks can include security incidents and data breaches or disclosures. A security incident may be defined as any event that compromises a security attribute (confidentiality, integrity, availability) of an information asset. A data breach or disclosure may be defined as any event resulting in confirmed compromise (unauthorized viewing or accessing) of any non-public information. See table 2 above for a list of selected cyber attacks.

[2] We anticipate that this report will be the first in a series examining cybersecurity in the banking and finance sector. As a result, this report addresses policy-level cybersecurity issues facing depository institutions and only briefly discusses operational-level cyber threats to depository institutions, such as payment systems, equities, and other similar issues. Also, this report does not address cyber threats to the securities, insurance, and other industries within the banking and finance sector.

[3] In this report, we refer to the regulators of depository institutions (banks, thrifts, and credit unions), and their holding companies as bank regulators. The Bureau of Consumer Financial Protection is responsible for examining depository institutions with total assets greater than $10 billion for compliance with consumer protection laws, but we did not review the Bureau's activities for this report.

[4] See GAO, *Critical Infrastructure Protection: Cybersecurity Guidance Is Available, but More Can Be Done to Promote Its Use*, GAO-12-92 (Washington, D.C.: Dec. 9, 2011), for our comparison of the FFIEC IT Examination Handbook to National Institute of Standards and Technology, *Recommended Security Controls for Federal Information Systems and Organizations*, Special Publication 800-53, Rev. 3 (Gaithersburg, Md.; May 2010).

[5] To ensure that we got examples of the large, mid-sized, and small-sized institutions at each of the four regulators, we used the following asset size categories for depository institutions regulated by the Federal Deposit Insurance Corporation, the Board of Governors of the Federal Reserve, and the Office of the Comptroller of the Currency: small banks—less than $1 billion; medium—$1 billion to less than $10 billion; large— $10 billion or more in assets. For credit unions regulated by the National Credit Union Administration, we broke up institutions according to the following asset categories: small credit unions—less than $10 million; medium—$10 million to less than $100 million; large—$100 million or more in assets. However, because even the large institutions overseen by some of these regulators still may be only medium or small in size when compared to all institutions, for reporting purposes we organized the institutions we selected into categories that better reflect the total size ranges of institutions, including categorizing institutions as large if they had assets of $50 billion or more; as medium if they had assets from $1 billion to less than $50 billion; and as small, for those with assets of less than $1 billion.

[6] GAO, *Standards for Internal Control in the Federal Government*, GAO/AIMD-00.21.3.1 (Washington, D.C.: November 1999).

[7] BITS is not an acronym. At one time, BITS stood for "Banking Industry Technology Secretariat." BITS is the technology policy division of the Financial Services Roundtable.

[8] GAO, *Information Sharing: Practices That Can Benefit Critical Infrastructure Protection*, GAO-02-24 (Washington, D.C.: Oct. 15, 2001); *Information Sharing: DHS Has*

Demonstrated Leadership and Progress, but Additional Actions Could Help Sustain and Strengthen Efforts, GAO-12-809 (Washington, D.C.: Sept. 18, 2012); and *DHS Intelligence Analysis: Additional Actions Needed to Address Analytic Priorities and Workforce Challenges*, GAO-14-397 (Washington, D.C.: June 4, 2014).

In: Cybersecurity and Information Security … ISBN: 978-1-63484-285-3
Editor: Lauren Hubbard

Chapter 2

INFORMATION SECURITY: FDIC IMPLEMENTED MANY CONTROLS OVER FINANCIAL SYSTEMS, BUT OPPORTUNITIES FOR IMPROVEMENT REMAIN*

United States Government Accountability Office

ABBREVIATIONS

DIF	Deposit Insurance Fund
FDIC	Federal Deposit Insurance Corporation
FIPS	Federal Information Processing Standard
FISMA	Federal Information Security Management Act of 2002
FRF	Federal Savings and Loan Insurance Corporation Resolution Fund
IT	information technology
NIST	National Institute of Standards and Technology
POA&M	plan of action and milestones
SP	special publication
US-CERT	United States Computer Emergency Readiness Team

* This is an edited, reformatted and augmented version of The United States Government Accountability Office publication, GAO-15-426, dated April 2015.

WHY GAO DID THIS STUDY

FDIC has a demanding responsibility enforcing banking laws, regulating financial institutions, and protecting depositors. Because of the importance of FDIC's work, effective information security controls are essential to ensure that the corporation's systems and information are adequately protected from inadvertent or deliberate misuse, improper modification, unauthorized disclosure, or destruction.

As part of its audits of the 2014 financial statements of the Deposit Insurance Fund and the Federal Savings and Loan Insurance Corporation Resolution Fund administered by FDIC, GAO assessed the effectiveness of the corporation's controls in protecting the confidentiality, integrity, and availability of its financial systems and information. To do so, GAO examined security policies, procedures, reports, and other documents; tested controls over key financial applications; and interviewed FDIC personnel.

WHAT GAO RECOMMENDS

GAO is making two recommendations to FDIC to improve its implementation of its information security program. FDIC concurred with GAO's recommendations. In a separate report with limited distribution, GAO is recommending that FDIC take five specific actions to address weaknesses in security controls.

WHAT GAO FOUND

The Federal Deposit Insurance Corporation (FDIC) has implemented numerous information security controls intended to protect its key financial systems; nevertheless, weaknesses remain that place the confidentiality, integrity, and availability of financial systems and information at risk. During 2014, the corporation implemented 27 of the 36 GAO recommendations pertaining to previously reported security weaknesses that were unaddressed as of December 31, 2013; actions to implement the remaining 9 recommendations were in progress. The table below details the status of these recommendations.

Status of Previously Reported Information Security Recommendations

Year reported		Not implemented at the beginning of 2014	Implemented during 2014	Actions in progress
	2010	1[a]	1	0
	2012	1 [b]	1	0
	2013	9[c]	6	3
	2014	25	19	6
Total		36	27	9

Source: GAO analysis of FDIC data. | GAO-15-426.

[a] FDIC had previously implemented 32 of the 33 recommendations GAO originally reported in 2010.

[b] FDIC had previously implemented 41 of the 42 recommendations GAO originally reported in 2012.

[c] FDIC had previously implemented 21 of the 30 recommendations GAO originally reported in 2013.

Although FDIC developed and implemented elements of its information security program, shortcomings remain in key program activities. For example:

- FDIC had taken steps to improve its security policies and procedures but important activities were not always required by its policies. For example, although FDIC had a policy on controlling physical access to its primary data center, the policy did not apply to all FDIC data centers.
- FDIC did not consistently remediate agency-identified weaknesses in a timely manner. However, to its credit, the corporation created a strategy outlining planned actions to address weaknesses in its remedial action processes.

Additionally, FDIC has designed and documented numerous information security controls intended to protect its key financial systems; nevertheless, controls were not always consistently implemented. For example, the corporation had not always (1) ensured that passwords for a financial application complied with FDIC policy for password length or (2) centrally collected audit logs on certain servers.

These weaknesses individually or collectively do not constitute either a material weakness or a significant deficiency for financial reporting purposes. Nonetheless, by mitigating known information security weaknesses and consistently applying information security controls, FDIC could continue to reduce risks and better protect its sensitive financial information and resources from inadvertent or deliberate misuse, improper modification, unauthorized disclosure, or destruction.

* * *

April 9, 2015

The Honorable Martin J. Gruenberg Chairman
Federal Deposit Insurance Corporation

Dear Chairman Gruenberg:

The Federal Deposit Insurance Corporation (FDIC) has a demanding responsibility enforcing banking laws, regulating banking institutions, and protecting depositors. In carrying out its financial and mission-related operations, FDIC relies extensively on computerized systems. Because the corporation plays an important role in maintaining public confidence in the nation's financial system, issues that affect the confidentiality, integrity, and availability of the sensitive information maintained on its systems are of paramount concern. In particular, effective information security controls are essential to ensure that FDIC systems and information are being adequately protected from inadvertent or deliberate misuse, fraudulent use, improper disclosure, or destruction.

As part of our audit of FDIC's 2014 financial statements of the Deposit Insurance Fund and the Federal Savings and Loan Insurance Corporation Resolution Fund, we assessed the effectiveness of FDIC's information security controls over key financial systems, data, and networks.[1] In our audit report, we concluded that FDIC maintained, in all material respects, effective internal control over financial reporting as of December 31, 2014, based on criteria established under the Federal Managers' Financial Integrity Act of 1982.[2]

In this report, we provide additional details on FDIC's information security controls over its computerized financial systems during 2014. Our objective was to determine the effectiveness of the corporation's controls in protecting the confidentiality, integrity, and availability of its financial systems and information. To do this, we examined FDIC information security policies, plans, and procedures; tested controls over its key financial applications; reviewed our prior reports to identify previously reported weaknesses and assess the effectiveness of corrective actions taken; and interviewed agency officials. This work was performed to support our opinion on FDIC's internal control over financial reporting as of December 31, 2014.

We performed our work in accordance with U.S. generally accepted government auditing standards. We believe that our audit work provided a reasonable basis for our conclusion in this report. See appendix I for more details on our objective, scope, and methodology.

BACKGROUND

Information security is a critical consideration for any agency that depends on information systems and computer networks to carry out its mission and is especially important for a government corporation such as FDIC, which has responsibilities to oversee the financial institutions that are entrusted with safeguarding the public's money. While the use of interconnected electronic information systems allows the corporation to accomplish its mission more quickly and effectively, this also exposes FDIC's information to threats from sources internal and external to the agency. Internal threats include errors, as well as fraudulent or malevolent acts by employees or contractors working within the agency. External threats include the ever-growing number of cyber-based attacks that can come from a variety of sources such as hackers, criminals, foreign nations, terrorists, and other adversarial groups.

Potential cyber attackers have a variety of techniques at their disposal, which can vastly enhance the reach and impact of their actions. For example, cyber attackers do not need to be physically close to their targets, their attacks can easily cross state and national borders, and they can preserve their anonymity. Additionally, advanced persistent threats— where an adversary that possesses sophisticated levels of expertise and significant resources can attack using physical and cyber methods to achieve its objectives[3] — pose increasing risks. Further, the interconnectivity among information systems presents increasing opportunities for such attacks. Indeed, reports of security incidents from federal agencies are on the rise. Specifically, the number of incidents reported by federal agencies to the United States Computer Emergency Readiness Team[4] (US-CERT) has increased dramatically in recent years: from 5,503 incidents reported in fiscal year 2006 to 67,168 incidents in fiscal year 2014.

Compounding the growing number and types of threats are the deficiencies in security controls on the information systems at federal agencies, which have resulted in vulnerabilities in both financial and nonfinancial systems and information. These deficiencies continue to place assets at risk of inadvertent or deliberate misuse, financial information at risk of unauthorized modification or destruction, and critical operations at risk of disruption. Accordingly, we have designated information security as a government-wide high-risk area since 1997, a designation that remains in force today. [5]

Federal law and guidance specify requirements for protecting federal information and information systems. The Federal Information Security Management Act of 2002 (FISMA)[6] provides a comprehensive framework for ensuring the effectiveness of information security controls over information resources that support federal operations and assets. To accomplish this, FISMA requires each agency to develop, document, and implement an agency-wide information security program to provide information security for the information and systems that support its operations and assets, using a risk-based approach to information security management. Such a program includes assessing risk; developing and implementing cost-effective security plans, policies, and procedures; providing specialized training; testing and evaluating the effectiveness of controls; planning, implementing, evaluating, and documenting remedial actions to address information security deficiencies; and ensuring continuity of operations.

FISMA also assigned to the National Institute of Standards and Technology (NIST) the responsibility for developing standards and guidelines that include minimum information security requirements. To this end, NIST has issued several publications to provide guidance for agencies in implementing an information security program. For example, NIST Federal Information Processing Standard (FIPS) 199[7] provides requirements on how agencies should categorize their information and information system(s) and NIST special publication (SP) 800-53[8] provides guidance to agencies on the selection and implementation of information security and privacy controls for systems.

FDIC Is a Key Protector of Bank and Thrift Deposits

FDIC was created by Congress to maintain the stability of and public confidence in the nation's financial system by insuring deposits, examining and supervising financial institutions, and resolving troubled institutions. FDIC is an independent agency of the federal government, which Congress created in 1933[9] in response to the thousands of bank failures that had occurred throughout the late 1920s and early 1930s.[10] FDIC insures deposits in banks and thrift institutions for at least $250,000; identifies, monitors, and addresses risks to the deposit insurance funds; and limits the effect on the economy and the financial system when a bank or thrift institution fails.

FDIC administers two funds in carrying out its mission:

- The Deposit Insurance Fund (DIF) has the primary purposes of (1) insuring the deposits and protecting the depositors of banks and savings associations (insured depository institutions) and (2) resolving failed insured depository institutions in a manner that will result in the least possible cost to the fund. In cooperation with other federal and state agencies, FDIC promotes the safety and soundness of insured depository institutions by identifying, monitoring, and addressing risks to the DIF.
- The Federal Savings and Loan Insurance Corporation Resolution Fund (FRF) is responsible for the sale of the remaining assets and the satisfaction of the liabilities associated with the former Federal Savings and Loan Insurance Corporation and the former Resolution Trust Corporation.

FDIC maintains the DIF and the FRF separately to support their respective functions.[11]

FDIC Relies on Computer Systems to Support Its Mission and Financial Reporting

FDIC relies extensively on computerized systems to support its mission, including financial operations, and to store the sensitive information that it collects. The corporation uses local and wide area networks to interconnect its systems and a layered approach to security defense.

To support its financial management functions, FDIC uses

- a corporate-wide system that functions as a unified set of financial and payroll systems that are managed and operated in an integrated fashion;

- a system to calculate and collect FDIC deposit insurance premiums and Financing Corporation[12] bond principal and interest amounts from insured financial institutions;
- a web-based application that provides full functionality to support franchise marketing, asset marketing, and asset management;
- an application and web portal to provide acquiring institutions with a secure method for submitting required data files to FDIC;
- computer programs used to derive the corporation's estimate of losses from shared loss agreements;
- a system to request access to and receive permission for the computer applications and resources available to its employees, contractors, and other authorized personnel; and
- a primary receivership and subsidiary financial processing and reporting system.

Under FISMA, the Chairman of FDIC is responsible for, among other things,

- providing information security protections commensurate with the risk and magnitude of the harm resulting from unauthorized access, use, disclosure, disruption, modification, or destruction of the agency's information systems and information;
- ensuring that senior agency officials provide information security for the information and information systems that support the operations and assets under their control; and
- delegating to the corporation's Chief Information Officer the authority to ensure compliance with the requirements imposed on the agency under FISMA.

The Chief Information Officer is responsible for developing and maintaining a corporate-wide information security program and for developing and maintaining information security policies, procedures, and control techniques that address all applicable requirements. The Chief Information Officer also serves as the authorizing official with the authority to approve the operation of the information systems at an acceptable level of risk to the corporation.

The Chief Information Security Officer reports to the Chief Information Officer and serves as the Chief Information Officer's designated representative. The Chief Information Security Officer is responsible for (1) the overall support of assessment and authorization activities; (2) the development, coordination, and implementation of FDIC's security policy; and (3) the coordination of information security and privacy efforts across the corporation.

FDIC Had Developed and Documented Many Controls to Secure Its Financial Information and Systems, but Improvements Are Still Needed

Although FDIC developed and implemented elements of its information security program, the corporation did not always implement key program activities. Additionally, FDIC has designed and documented numerous information security controls intended to protect its key financial systems; however, shortcomings existed in the implementation of other information security controls. By mitigating known information security weaknesses and ensuring that information security controls are consistently applied, FDIC could continue to reduce risks and better protect its sensitive financial information and resources from inadvertent or deliberate misuse, improper modification, unauthorized disclosure, or destruction.

FDIC Continues to Make Progress in Implementing Its Information Security Program

An entity-wide information security management program is the foundation of a security control structure and a reflection of senior management's commitment to addressing security risks. The security management program should establish a framework and continuous cycle of activity for assessing risk, developing and implementing effective security procedures, and monitoring the effectiveness of these procedures. Without a well-designed program, security controls may be inadequate; responsibilities may be unclear, misunderstood, or improperly implemented; and controls may be inconsistently applied. FISMA requires each agency to develop, document, and implement an information security program that, among other things, includes

- plans for providing adequate information security for networks, facilities, and systems;
- security awareness training to inform personnel of information security risks and of their responsibilities in complying with agency policies and procedures, as well as training personnel with significant security responsibilities for information security;
- policies and procedures that (1) are based on risk assessments, (2) cost effectively reduce information security risks to an acceptable level, (3) ensure that information security is addressed throughout the life cycle of each system, and (4) ensure compliance with applicable requirements;
- a process for planning, implementing, evaluating, and documenting remedial actions to address any deficiencies in its information security policies, procedures, or practices; and
- periodic testing and evaluation of the effectiveness of information security policies, procedures, and practices, to be performed with a frequency depending on risk, but no less than annually, and that includes testing of management, operational, and technical controls for every system identified in the agency's required inventory of major information systems.

FDIC Developed and Documented Elements of Its Corporate Information Security Program

FDIC made improvements in developing and documenting many elements of its corporate information security program. For example:

- During 2014, FDIC completed actions to address two weaknesses we previously reported related to system security planning. Specifically, the corporation had ensured that the system security plans for three applications thoroughly described each control and included all required information, and ensured that descriptions of common controls were adequately documented.
- During 2014, FDIC addressed our prior recommendation to ensure that those with administrative-level access have completed the requisite rules of behavior training upon receiving access and each year after that.
- FDIC had taken steps to document, implement, and improve policies for information security. Specifically, in June 2014, the corporation

formalized a new policy on security patch management. The policy defines risk categories for patches, time frames for applying patches based on the risk categories and platform-specific requirements, and roles and responsibilities for patch management. Additionally, the FDIC Office of the Inspector General reported in November 2014 that FDIC had drafted a new information technology (IT) security risk management program policy that was designed to align with NIST and Office of Management and Budget guidance and reflect the corporation's information security risk management program and governance structure.

- FDIC addressed many weaknesses that we previously identified in its information systems supporting financial processing. Specifically, during 2014, FDIC implemented 27 of the 36 recommendations pertaining to unaddressed security weaknesses that we previously reported, and actions to correct or mitigate the remaining 9 weaknesses were in progress.

Information Security Program Continues to Present Opportunities for Improvement

Although FDIC continues to improve its implementation of its corporate information security program, shortcomings existed in other information security program elements. Specifically:

- FDIC's information security policies and procedures did not always include important requirements. NIST special publication (SP) 800-53 Revision 4 recommends that agencies regularly review individuals' physical access to facilities and remove that access when it is no longer required. However, although FDIC had a policy on controlling physical access to its primary data center, the corporation did not recertify access to its backup data center because the policy did not apply to all FDIC data centers. Additionally, although FDIC policy states that access to IT resources is to be provided only after proper authorization has been provided, the corporation did not document that it had verified access to a system supporting the marketing of failed banks' assets because its existing procedures did not require the access verifications to be documented. As a result, there is an increased risk that individuals who no longer need access to information systems could accidentally or intentionally damage critical resources.

- Improvements are needed in the corporation's continuous monitoring program. To its credit, the corporation conducted control assessments of the major applications and general support systems we reviewed and addressed a weakness we previously identified by assessing security controls for two systems in accordance with its assessment schedule. In addition, the FDIC Office of Inspector General reported in November 2014 that FDIC had performed a number of continuous monitoring activities, developed an assessment methodology that defined a risk-focused approach for performing continuous monitoring on information systems, and reported various continuous monitoring metrics to senior managers. However, the office reported that the corporation had not yet developed a written, corporate-wide information security continuous monitoring strategy that included key elements from NIST guidance for continuous monitoring. The office recommended that FDIC develop and approve a written continuous monitoring strategy consistent with Office of Management and Budget and NIST guidance. Until this recommendation is addressed, FDIC will have limited assurance that the controls are operating effectively to protect its financial systems and information.
- Improvements are needed in the corporation's remedial action processes. Specifically, at the time of our review, 25 of the 285 remedial action plans applicable to agency information systems in our audit scope were past their expected closure dates by between about 2 weeks and 10 months, including 4 high-risk items. In addition, the FDIC Office of Inspector General reported in November 2014 that, as of July 2014, the corporation's remedial action management system contained a large number of high- and moderate-risk security vulnerabilities, many of which had planned corrective actions that were significantly past their scheduled completion dates. The Office also reported that FDIC has taken steps to improve its remedial action processes by creating a strategy outlining planned actions to address weaknesses in the corporation's plan of action and milestones processes. Nevertheless, until FDIC fully addresses shortcomings in its remedial action processes, the corporation's financial information and systems will remain at increased and unnecessary risk. Because the FDIC Office of Inspector General has already made recommendations to address shortcomings in FDIC's remedial action processes, we are not making additional recommendations in this area.

FDIC Implemented Many Controls, but Shortcomings Still Warrant Management Attention

An agency can protect the resources that support its critical operations and assets from unauthorized access, disclosure, modification, or loss by designing and implementing controls for segregating incompatible duties, identifying and authenticating users, restricting user access to only what has been authorized, encrypting sensitive data, auditing and monitoring systems to detect potentially malicious activity, managing and controlling system configurations, and conducting employee background investigations, among other things. Although FDIC had implemented numerous controls in these areas, weaknesses continue to challenge the corporation in ensuring the confidentiality, integrity, and availability of its information and information systems.

Controls for Segregation of Incompatible Duties Improved

To reduce the risk of error or fraud, duties and responsibilities for authorizing, processing, recording, and reviewing transactions should be separated to ensure that one user does not control all of the critical stages of a process. NIST SP 800-53 Revision 4 states that, to prevent malevolent activity without collusion, organizations should separate the duties of users as necessary and implement separation of duties through defined information system access authorizations. Additionally, consistent with NIST guidance, FDIC policy on access control for IT resources states that, where required, access controls shall be used to enforce the principle of separation of duties to restrict the level of access and ability provided to any single user.

FDIC improved its implementation of segregation of duties controls by implementing four recommendations we had previously made pertaining to segregation of duties. For example, FDIC identified and documented incompatible roles and established processes and procedures to enforce segregation of duties for several applications and systems supporting financial processing. Additionally, the corporation had restricted users with access to source code for a financial system from having access to that system's production environment. As a result, FDIC has reduced its risk that users could conduct fraudulent activity by bypassing intended controls.

Improvements Made in Controls for Identifying and Authenticating Users, but Password Controls Were Not Always Implemented

Information systems need to effectively control user accounts and identify and authenticate users. Users and devices should be appropriately identified and authenticated through the implementation of adequate logical access controls. Users can be authenticated using mechanisms such as a password and user ID combination. Consistent with NIST SP 800-53 Revision 4, FDIC policy establishes minimum password length and complexity requirements.

During 2014, FDIC improved controls for identifying and authenticating the identity of users by implementing two recommendations that we had previously made and that were still unresolved as of December 31, 2013. For example, FDIC had disallowed the use of default credentials for access to an application supporting FDIC's process for managing cash and investment transactions and had provided password lifetime and complexity controls to user accounts for a database that supported financial processing.

However, FDIC did not fully implement password controls on the application supporting its process for managing cash and investment transactions in accordance with its policy. Specifically, passwords for the application did not comply with the minimum length standards established by FDIC's password policy. As a result, there is an increased likelihood that passwords could potentially be compromised and used to gain unauthorized access to financial information in the application.

Controls for Restricting Access to Only What Users Needed Were Largely Effective, but Shortcomings Remain

Authorization encompasses access privileges granted to a user, program, or process. It is used to allow or prevent actions by that user based on predefined rules. Authorization includes the principles of legitimate use and least privilege.[13] NIST SP 800-53 Revision 4 recommends that organizations employ the principle of least privilege by allowing only authorized access for users (or processes acting on behalf of users) which are necessary to accomplish assigned tasks in accordance with organizational missions and business functions, periodically review the privileges assigned to users to validate the need for such privileges and reassign or remove privileges when necessary, and disable access to information systems within a defined period when individuals are terminated. NIST also recommends that organizations develop, approve, and maintain a list of individuals with authorized access to facilities where information systems reside, periodically review the list, and remove individuals from the list when access to the facility is no longer required. Consistent with NIST guidance, FDIC policy also states that access to IT resources shall be terminated immediately after an employee or contractor exits the FDIC and that periodic reviews of access settings shall be conducted to ensure that appropriate controls remain consistent with existing authorizations and current business needs.

During 2014, FDIC improved controls for authorizing users' access by implementing 11 of 12 recommendations we had previously made pertaining to authorization controls and that were still unresolved as of December 31, 2013. For example, FDIC had

- ensured that accounts belonging to users who had not accessed certain applications and systems in a predefined period of time were disabled,
- discontinued the use of shared user IDs for several applications and databases supporting financial processing,
- removed certain users' excessive access to an application supporting FDIC's process for estimating potential losses from litigation, and
- restricted access to the network shared folder where annual financial statements and footnotes were maintained.

Although improvements were made, FDIC did not always implement sufficient authorization controls. For example, as discussed earlier, the corporation did not recertify the need for data center access on a periodic basis to ensure that individuals' access remained appropriate, and did not always recertify account access to an application used by FDIC to store loan data for failing financial institutions. Additionally, the corporation had not yet completed actions to implement our prior-year recommendation to ensure that accounts for users who have access to the network and who have been separated from employment are removed immediately upon separation.

Although these weaknesses did not materially impact FDIC's financial statements, they nevertheless increase the risk that individuals may have greater access to data centers or to financial information and systems than they need to fulfill their responsibilities, or that user accounts for departed individuals could be used to gain unauthorized access to systems that process sensitive financial information.

FDIC Used Strong Encryption for Two Systems, but Did Not Always Sufficiently Encrypt Sensitive Connections

Cryptography controls can be used to help protect the integrity and confidentiality of data and computer programs by rendering data unintelligible to unauthorized users and/or protecting the integrity of transmitted or stored data. Cryptography involves the use of mathematical functions called algorithms and strings of seemingly random bits called keys to, among other things, encrypt a message or file so that it is unintelligible to those who do not have the secret key needed to decrypt it, thus keeping the contents of the message or file confidential. NIST Special Publication 800-53 Revision 4 recommends that organizations employ cryptographic mechanisms to prevent unauthorized disclosure of information during transmission, encrypt passwords while being stored and transmitted, and establish a trusted communications path between users and security functions of information systems. The NIST standard for an encryption algorithm is Federal Information Processing Standard (FIPS) 140-2.[14]

FDIC improved its encryption controls by implementing our prior-year recommendation to use FIPS 140-2-compliant encryption for protection of authentication and session data for two systems supporting financial processing. However, FDIC had not completed actions to implement our prior recommendation to use FIPS-compliant encryption for all mainframe connections. As a result, sensitive data transmitted over these connections could be exposed to potential compromise.

Audit and Monitoring Controls Improved, but Opportunities for Improvement Remain

Audit and monitoring involves the regular collection, review, and analysis of auditable events for indications of inappropriate or unusual activity, and the appropriate investigation and reporting of such activity. Automated mechanisms may be used to integrate audit monitoring, analysis, and reporting into an overall process for investigation and response to suspicious activities. Audit and monitoring controls can help security professionals routinely assess computer security, perform investigations during and after an attack, and even recognize an ongoing attack. Audit and monitoring technologies include network and host-based intrusion detection systems, audit logging, security event correlation tools, and computer forensics. NIST SP 800-53 revision 4 states that organizations should review and analyze information system audit records for indications of inappropriate or unusual activity and report the findings to designated agency officials. Additionally, NIST states that audit records should contain information on individual audit events, including their type, source, and outcome, as well as the date and time that they occurred and any individuals or subjects associated with the events, among other things.

FDIC improved its audit and monitoring controls by implementing three of six recommendations pertaining to audit and monitoring that we had previously identified and that were still unresolved as of December 31, 2013. For example, the corporation had ensured that log history for privileged accounts on key servers supporting financial processing were sufficient to aid incident response and forensic investigations.

However, FDIC had not yet completed actions to address three weaknesses related to auditing and monitoring controls we previously identified. For example, the corporation had not yet ensured that, for certain systems, sensitive and high-risk events are consistently logged. In addition, FDIC did not always effectively monitor server security logs. Specifically, three servers supporting financial processing did not send log output to the corporation's centralized audit logging system.

While the three outstanding recommendations and the additional weakness identified this year did not materially affect the corporation's financial statements, they nevertheless increase the risk that the incident response team would not detect malicious activity occurring on these systems supporting financial processing, or that sufficient data would not be available, hindering efforts to investigate potential security incidents after the fact.

Configuration Management Shortcomings Increase Risk to Financial Systems and Information

Configuration management is an important control that involves the identification and management of security features for all hardware and software components of an information system at a given point and systematically controls changes to that configuration during the system's life cycle. Configuration management involves, among other things, (1) verifying the correctness of the security settings in the operating systems, applications, or computing and network devices and (2) obtaining reasonable assurance that systems are configured and operating securely and as intended. Patch management, a component of configuration management, is important for mitigating the risks associated with software vulnerabilities. When a software vulnerability is discovered, the software vendor may develop and distribute a patch or work-around to mitigate the vulnerability. Without the patch, an attacker can exploit the vulnerability to read, modify, or delete sensitive information; disrupt operations; or launch attacks against other systems.

NIST SP 800-53 Revision 4 states that organizations should establish a baseline configuration for the information system and its constituent components. Additionally, FDIC policy states that FDIC must establish and document mandatory configuration settings for IT products employed within the information system using information-system-defined security configuration checklists. Further, NIST SP 800-128[15] states that patch management procedures should define how the organization's patch management process is integrated into configuration management processes, how patches are prioritized and approved through the configuration change control process, and how patches are tested for their impact on existing secure configurations.

Although improvements were made, shortcomings remain in FDIC's implementation of configuration management controls. FDIC had made progress toward addressing our prior recommendation to establish baseline configurations for all FDIC information systems by establishing agency-wide configuration settings for three platforms. According to officials, FDIC plans to establish baselines for the majority of its platforms by the end of 2015. In addition, FDIC had begun to implement actions intended to improve its process for managing vulnerabilities and applying patches, including establishing a Patch and Vulnerability Group to facilitate the identification and distribution of patches; however, the corporation had not yet completed actions to address our prior recommendation to apply patches to remediate known vulnerabilities in third-party software.

These issues did not materially affect the corporation's financial statements. Nevertheless, until our previously identified weaknesses are addressed, FDIC faces increased risk that unpatched vulnerabilities in systems and applications could be exploited, potentially exposing the corporation's financial systems and information to unauthorized access or modification.

FDIC Had Not Yet Corrected Employee Background Investigation Issue

Policies related to hiring and management of personnel are important considerations in securing information systems. If personnel policies are not adequate, an entity runs the risk of (1) hiring unqualified or untrustworthy individuals; (2) providing terminated employees opportunities to sabotage or otherwise impair entity operations or assets; (3) failing to detect continuing unauthorized employee actions; (4) lowering employee morale, which may in turn diminish employee compliance with controls; and (5) allowing staff expertise to decline. Personnel procedures should include contacting references, performing background investigations, and ensuring that periodic reinvestigations are consistent with the sensitivity of the position, in accordance with criteria from the Office of Personnel Management. FDIC policy states that personnel in moderate- and low-risk positions should be subject to a background reinvestigation every 5 and 7 years, respectively.

In 2014, we reported that background reinvestigations were not being performed in accordance with FDIC policy; specifically, background reinvestigations had not been performed prior to Fall 2013 for users with a security rating less than high risk. During our current review, FDIC officials stated that their planned efforts to address this weakness will not be completed until April 2016. Until this weakness is fully addressed, FDIC will continue to face elevated risk that it will not identify malicious users of financial applications who would commit or attempt to commit fraud.

CONCLUSION

FDIC had developed, documented, and implemented many elements of its corporate information security program. For example, the corporation had formalized a new policy for information security patch management and had ensured that administrators completed required training. In addition, FDIC had implemented and strengthened many information security controls over its financial systems and information. For example, the corporation had taken steps to improve controls for segregating incompatible duties, identifying and authenticating users, restricting user access to only what has been authorized, encrypting of sensitive data, and auditing and monitoring systems for potentially malicious activity, by addressing many of the weaknesses that we previously reported.

However, management attention is still needed to address shortcomings in the corporation's information security program. For example, shortcomings in certain security policies and procedures led to weaknesses in conducting and documenting reviews of user access. Additionally, further actions are needed to address weaknesses in identification and authentication, authorization, and audit and monitoring controls. Given the important role that information systems play in FDIC's internal controls over financial reporting, it is vitally important that FDIC address the remaining weaknesses in information security controls—both old and new—as part of its ongoing efforts to mitigate the risks from cyber attacks and to ensure the confidentiality, integrity, and availability of its financial and sensitive information. Although we do not consider these weaknesses individually or collectively to be either a material weakness or a significant deficiency for financial reporting purposes, we are nevertheless making five recommendations in a separate product with limited distribution for FDIC to address new weaknesses we identified in this review. Until FDIC takes further steps to mitigate these weaknesses, the corporation's sensitive financial information and resources will remain unnecessarily exposed to increased risk of inadvertent or deliberate misuse, improper modification, unauthorized disclosure, or destruction.

RECOMMENDATIONS FOR EXECUTIVE ACTION

To help improve the corporation's implementation of its information security program, we recommend that the Chairman of FDIC direct the Chief Information Officer to take the following two actions:

- Ensure that physical access policies require periodic review of access to all FDIC data centers.
- Update existing procedures to require that access verifications to the system supporting the marketing of failed banks' assets be documented.

Additionally, in a separate report with limited distribution, we are making five recommendations consisting of actions to implement and correct specific information security weaknesses related to identification and authentication, authorization, and audit and monitoring.

AGENCY COMMENTS

In providing written comments on a draft of this report, FDIC stated that corrective actions for the two new recommendations have already been or will be completed during 2015. FDIC also provided an attachment detailing its actions to implement our recommendations as well as technical comments that we addressed in our report as appropriate.

Gregory C. Wilshusen
Director, Information Security Issues

Dr. Nabajyoti Barkakati
Director, Center for Science, Technology, and Engineering

APPENDIX I: OBJECTIVE, SCOPE AND METHODOLOGY

The objective of this information security review was to determine the effectiveness of the Federal Deposit Insurance Corporation's (FDIC) controls in protecting the confidentiality, integrity, and availability of its financial systems and information. The review was conducted as part of our audit of the FDIC financial statements of the Deposit Insurance Fund and the Federal Savings and Loan Insurance Corporation Resolution Fund.

The scope of our audit included an examination of FDIC information security policies and plans; controls over key financial systems; and interviews with agency officials in order to (1) assess the effectiveness of corrective actions taken by FDIC to address weaknesses we previously reported and (2) determine whether any additional weaknesses existed. This work was performed in support of our opinion on internal control over financial reporting as it relates to our audits of the calendar year 2014 and 2013 financial statements of the two funds administered by FDIC.

GAO used an independent public accounting firm, under contract, to evaluate and test certain FDIC information systems controls, including the follow-up on the status of FDIC's corrective actions during calendar year 2014 to address open recommendations from our prior years' reports. We agreed on the scope of the audit work, monitored the firm's progress, and reviewed the related audit documentation to determine whether the firm's findings were adequately supported.

To determine whether controls over key financial systems and information were effective, we considered the results FDIC's actions to mitigate previously reported weaknesses that remained open as of December 31, 2013, and performed audit work at FDIC facilities in Arlington, Virginia. We concentrated our evaluation primarily on the controls for systems and applications associated with financial processing. Our selection of the systems to evaluate was based on consideration of systems that directly or indirectly support the processing of material transactions that are reflected in the funds' financial statements.

Our audit methodology was based on the *Federal Information System Controls Audit Manual*,[1] which contains guidance for reviewing information system controls that affect the confidentiality, integrity, and availability of computerized information.

Using standards and guidance from the National Institute of Standards and Technology as well as FDIC's policies and procedures, we evaluated controls by

- examining access responsibilities to determine whether incompatible functions were segregated among different individuals;
- reviewed password settings to determine if password management was being enforced in accordance with agency policy;
- analyzing user system authorizations to determine whether users had more permissions than necessary to perform their assigned functions;
- observing methods for providing secure data transmissions to determine whether sensitive data were being encrypted;
- assessing configuration settings to evaluate settings used to audit security-relevant events; and
- inspecting vulnerability scans for in-scope systems to determine whether patches, service packs, and hot fixes were appropriately installed on affected systems.

Using the requirements of the Federal Information Security Management Act of 2002, which establishes elements for an agency-wide information security program, we evaluated FDIC's implementation of its security program by

- analyzing security plans for key financial systems to determine whether management, operational, and technical controls had been documented and whether security plans had been updated regularly in accordance with NIST requirements;
- reviewing training records for administrators to determine if they had received training appropriate to their responsibilities;
- reviewing information security policies to determine whether they were adequately documented and implemented;
- examining an FDIC Office of Inspector General report for information on FDIC's implementation of risk management policies;
- reviewing ongoing assessments of security controls to determine if they had been completed as scheduled;
- reviewing an FDIC Office of Inspector General report for information on the corporation's information security continuous monitoring program;
- examining remedial action plans to determine whether FDIC addressed identified vulnerabilities in a timely manner; and
- examining an FDIC Office of Inspector General report for information on findings related to FDIC's remedial action process.

To determine the status of FDIC's actions to correct or mitigate previously reported information security weaknesses, we reviewed prior GAO reports to identify previously reported weaknesses and examined FDIC's corrective action plans to determine which weaknesses FDIC had reported as being corrected. For those instances where FDIC reported it had completed corrective actions, we assessed the effectiveness of those actions.

We performed our work from June 2014 to April 2015 in accordance with U.S. generally accepted government auditing standards. We believe that our audit work provided a reasonable basis for our conclusion in this report.

End Notes

[1] GAO, Financial Audit: Federal Deposit Insurance Corporation Funds' 2014 and 2013 Financial Statements, GAO-15-289 (Washington, D.C.: Feb. 12, 2015).

[2] 31 U.S.C. § 3512(c) and (d).

[3] These objectives typically include establishing/extending footholds within the information technology infrastructure of the targeted agency for purposes of exfiltrating information undermining or impeding critical aspects of a mission, program, or agency; or positioning itself to carry out these objectives in the future. An advanced persistent threat (1) pursues its objectives repeatedly over an extended period of time, (2) adapts to defenders' efforts to resist it, and (3) maintains the level of interaction needed to achieve its objectives.

[4] The Department of Homeland Security's federal information security incident center is hosted by US-CERT. When incidents occur, agencies are to notify the center

[5] GAO, High-Risk Series: Information Management and Technology, GAO/HR-97-9 (Washington, D.C.: February 1997) and High Risk Series: An Update, GAO-15-290 (Washington, D.C.: February 2015).

[6] FISMA was enacted as title III, E-Government Act of 2002, Pub. L. No. 107-347, 116 Stat 2899, 2946 (Dec. 17, 2002). As our review was finishing, the Federal Information Security Modernization Act of 2014, Pub. L. No. 113-283 (Dec. 18, 2014) was enacted. However the new law, which partially supersedes FISMA, incorporates and continues the requirements from FISMA that we relied upon in our report. Accordingly, no changes to our findings were necessary.

[7] NIST, Standards for Security Categorization of Federal Information and Information Systems FIPS Publication 199 (Gaithersburg, Md.: February 2004).

[8] NIST, Security and Privacy Controls for Federal Information Systems and Organizations, SP 800-53, Revision 4 (Gaithersburg, Md.: April 2013).

[9] Federal Deposit Insurance Corporation Act, June 16, 1933, Ch. 89, § 8.

[10] FDIC receives no congressional appropriations; it is funded by premiums that banks and thrift institutions pay for deposit insurance coverage and from earnings on investments in U.S. Treasury securities.

[11] A third fund to be managed by FDIC, the Orderly Liquidation Fund, established by section 210 of the Dodd-Frank Wall Street Reform and Consumer Protection Act, Pub. L. No. 111-203, 124 Stat. 1376, 1506 (July 21, 2010), is unfunded and conducted no transactions during the fiscal years covered by this audit.

[12] The Financing Corporation, established by the Competitive Equality Banking Act of 1987, is a mixed-ownership government corporation whose primary purpose is to function as a financing vehicle for the Federal Savings and Loan Insurance Corporation. Effective December 12, 1991, as provided by the Resolution Trust Corporation Refinancing, Restructuring and Improvement Act of 1991, the Financing Corporation's ability to issue new debt was terminated. Outstanding Financing Corporation bonds, which are 30-year non-callable bonds with a principal amount of approximately $8.1 billion, mature in 2017 through 2019.

[13] Users should have the least amount of privileges (access to services) necessary to perform their duties.

[14] NIST, Security Requirements for Cryptographic Modules, FIPS 140-2 (Gaithersburg, Md.: May 2001).

[15] NIST, Guide for Security-Focused Configuration Management of Information Systems, SP 800-128 (Gaithersburg, Md.: August 2011).

End Note for Appendix I

[1] GAO, Federal Information System Controls Audit Manual (FISCAM), GAO-09-232G (Washington, D.C.: February 2009).

INDEX

A

B

C

D

E

N

O

P

Q

R

U

V

W